Cambridge IGCSE®
Complete
ICT

Third edition

OXFORD
UNIVERSITY PRESS

Great Clarendon Street, Oxford, OX2 6DP, United Kingdom

Oxford University Press is a department of the University of Oxford. It furthers the University's objective of excellence in research, scholarship, and education by publishing worldwide. Oxford is a registered trade mark of Oxford University Press in the UK and in certain other countries

First published in 2016

British Library Cataloguing in Publication Data
Data available

978-1-38-202283-5

1 3 5 7 9 10 8 6 4 2

Paper used in the production of this book is a natural, recyclable product made from wood grown in sustainable forests. The manufacturing process conforms to the environmental regulations of the country of origin.

Printed by CPI Group (UK) Ltd, Croydon CR0 4YY

Acknowledgements
The publisher and authors would like to thank the following for permission to use photographs and other copyright material:

Cover: MirageC/Getty Images. Photos: p6(q1): 300dpi/Shutterstock; p6(q2): R-studio/Shutterstock; p6(q3): jultud/Shutterstock; p7(q4): steamroller_blues/Shutterstock; p7(q5): Tom Wang/Shutterstock; p7(q6): Dennis Kitchen Studio, Inc/Oxford University Press; p7(q7): Volodymyr Krasyuk/Shutterstock; p8(q8): Serhii Fedoruk/Shutterstock; p8(q9): muse studio/Shutterstock; p8(q10): bogdandimages/Shutterstock; p19(q1): steamroller_blues/Shutterstock; p19(q2): Fazakas Mihaly/Shutterstock; p19(q3): Robert Milek/Shutterstock; p19(q4): Of I laugh/Shutterstock; p20(q5): Maksym Yemelyanov/123RF.com; p20(q6): Garsya/Shutterstock; p20(q7): Denis Dryashkin/Shutterstock; p20(q8): Bloomua/Shutterstock; p21(q9): Nataliia Mach/Alamy Stock Photo; p21(q10): MNI/Shutterstock; p28(q1): Vladimir Arndt/Shutterstock; p28(q2): HeartBeat/Shutterstock; p28(q3): Jaroslaw Grudzinski/Shutterstock; p29(q4): MyImages - Micha/Shutterstock; p29(q5): Garsya/Shutterstock; p54: terekhov igor/Shutterstock; p114: norazaminayob/Shutterstock; p178: mariakray/Shutterstock; p180(b): DG-Studio/Shutterstock.

All other images courtesy of Microsoft and Stephen Doyle.

Every effort has been made to contact copyright holders of material reproduced in this book. Any omissions will be rectified in subsequent printings if notice is given to the publisher.

Contents

Digital resources and syllabus matching grid

Welcome to your *Complete ICT for IGCSE® Teacher Resource Pack*.

The supporting website gives you access to all the activities data and documents to support the student activities in the *Complete ICT for IGCSE®* Third edition student book.

Topic title	IGCSE syllabus section	ICT Student Book page no.
Hardware and software	1.1	1
The main components of computer systems	1.2	3
Operating systems	1.3	4
Types of computer	1.4	6
Emerging technologies	1.5	7
Input devices and their uses	2.1	14
Direct data entry and associated devices	2.2	19
Output devices and their uses	2.3	23
Backing storage devices and media	3	31
Networks	4.1	38
Network devices	4.1	38
Setting up and configuring a small network	4.1	40
The internet	4.1	40
Intranets	4.1	41
Extranets	4.1	41
Types of network	4.1	42
Network issues and communication	4.2	43
The principles of a typical data protection act	8.2	47
Electronic conferencing	4.2	48
Microprocessor controlled devices	5.1	52
The potential health problems related to the prolonged use of IT equipment	5.2	54
Communication	6.1	58
Media streaming and e-publications	6.1	58
Measurement applications	6.2	59
Microprocessors in control applications	6.2	60
Modelling applications	6.2	62
Applications in manufacturing industries	6.3	63
School management systems	6.4	63
Booking systems	6.5	65
Banking applications	6.6	66
Computers in medicine	6.7	69
Computers in libraries	6.5	70
Expert systems	6.8	71
Computers in the retail industry	6.9	72
Recognition systems	6.10	74
Monitor and tracking systems	6.10	75
Satellite systems	6.11	76
The purpose of the systems life cycle	7.1	82
Analysis	7.1	82

Topic title	IGCSE syllabus section	ICT Student Book page no.
Design	7.2	84
Development and testing	7.3	85
Implementation	7.4	85
Documentation	7.5	86
Evaluation	7.6	88
Physical safety	8.1	92
Personal data	8.2	92
e-safety	8.2	93
Security of data	8.3	94
Audience appreciation	9.1	103
Copyright	9.2	104
Communication with other ICT users using email	10.1	107
Effective use of the internet	10.2	109
Managing files effectively	11.1	114
Reducing file sizes for storage or transmissions	11.2	117
Using software tools to position image	12	118
Using software tools to edit images	12	118
Create or edit a document	13.1	126
Tables	13.2	135
Headers and footers	13.3	137
The use and purpose of a corporate house style	14	140
Applying styles to ensure the consistency of presentation	14	140
Software tools	15.1	145
Proofing techniques	15.2	146
Producing graphs and charts from given data	16	149
Formatting text and organising page layout	17	168
Using software tools to edit tables	17	173
Creating a database structure	18.1	182
Manipulating data	18.2	199
Presenting data	18.3	207
Using a master slide to approximately place objects and set styles	19	236
Adding sound to a presentation	19	267
Adding movies (video clips and animated images) on the slide	19	269
Creating a controlled presentation	19	269
What is a data model	20.1	275
Creating a data mode1	20.1	275
Testing the data model	20.1	289
Manipulating data	20.2	290
Presenting data	20.3	301
Web development layers	21.1	305
HTML	21.2	305
Metatags	21.2	307
Creating an external stylesheet	21.3	307
Absolute and relative file paths	21.2	315
Using images on web pages	21.1	324
Use of the <div> tag to apply styles and classes	21.1	329
Adding audio (i.e. sound) to a webpage	21.1	332
Adding video to a webpage	21.1	333
Tables with default, collapsed and hidden borders	21.3	334

1 Types and components of computer systems

This worksheet can be best used following study of the hardware and software section in Chapter 1 on page 1 of the Student Book.

Worksheet 1.1

What is being shown here?

Here are some pieces of computer hardware or types of computer. You have to decide what name best describes the picture. To make things a little easier, here is a list of devices/types of computer to choose from.

scanner	**laptop computer**	**mouse**	**sound card**
desktop computer	**internal memory**	**fixed hard disk**	**motherboard**
processor	**tablet**		

1

Name: ______________________________

2

Name: ______________________________

3

Name: ______________________________

Worksheet 1.1 (continued)

4

Name:

5

Name:

6

Name:

7

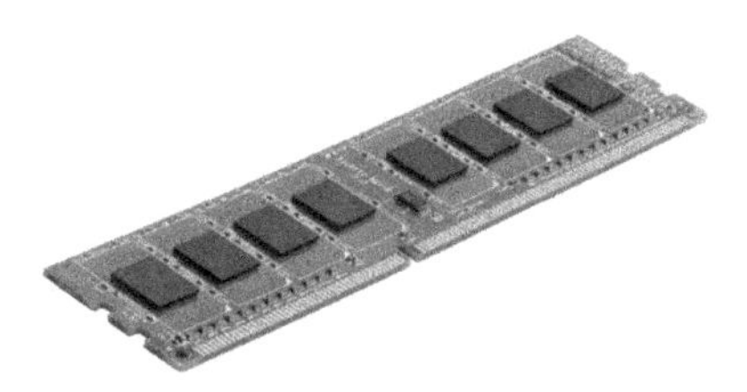

Name:

Worksheet 1.1 (continued)

8

Name:

9

Name:

10

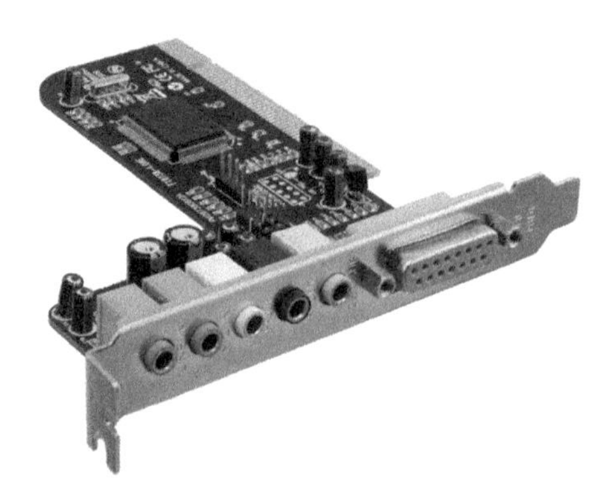

Name:

This worksheet can be best used following study of the hardware and software sections in Chapter 1 on pages 1 to 3 of the Student Book.

Worksheet 1.2

Hardware or software?

Here are some items that are either hardware or software. You have to decide which they are by putting a tick in the appropriate column.

	Name of item	Hardware	Software
1	Processor		
2	Operating system		
3	Fixed hard disk		
4	Memory chips (RAM and ROM)		
5	Keyboard		
6	Mouse		
7	Word processor		
8	Search engine		
9	Speakers		
10	Microphone		
11	DVD drive		
12	Blank DVD		
13	Database		
14	Spreadsheet		
15	Barcode reader		
16	Printer		
17	Web browser		
18	Removable hard disk		
19	Wireless router		
20	Digital camera		

This activity can best be completed after studying Chapter 1 pages 7 to 9 of the Student Book.

Activity 1.1

New technologies

There are many new technologies being developed and used in ICT.

You are required to write a short article for a newspaper about these technologies. Your audience may not have heard of them, so you need to ensure your article explains clearly what they are and why they have been developed.

Here are the technologies you should concentrate on:

- Autonomous vehicles
- Augmented reality
- Zero login
- Gesture-based interfaces

You should do some research on each of these first and obtain suitable images to include in your article.

Topic 1 answers

Questions A

Student book page 3

1 **a** One mark for:

Hardware – the physical parts of a computer that you can actually touch

One mark for:

Software – the sets of instructions that you cannot touch that tell the hardware how to operate

b One mark for two examples of hardware such as:

Keyboard

Mouse

Hard disk drive

CD/DVD drive

Internal memory (RAM and ROM)

Screen

etc.

One mark for two examples of software such as:

Systems software

Applications software

Operating system software

Device driver software

Word-processing software

Database software

Spreadsheet software

Photo-editing software

etc.

2 One mark for each answer.

a Operating system

b Utilities

c Operating system

d Operating system

e Utilities

f Device drivers

3 **a** One mark for each definition:

Internal hardware is hardware situated inside the computer casing.

External hardware is hardware situated outside the computer casing.

b One mark for each correctly placed item.

Internal hardware device	External hardware device
Motherboard	Mouse
Processor	Keyboard
ROM	Printer
Video card	
Internal hard disk drive	
RAM	
Sound card	

4 **a** One mark each for two reasons such as:

To provide a user interface (i.e. a way for the user to interact with the computer)

To control the system resources and the processing

To handle inputs and outputs

To handle the storage of data

To maximise the use of computer memory

To handle interrupts and decide what action to take

b **i** One mark for software

ii Used to supply the instructions to the computer to instruct it how to use the attached printer

c One mark each for two of the following:

File maintenance tasks

Compressing files

Installing and uninstalling software

Compacting files on the hard disk

Finding and removing viruses

Burning CDs and DVDs

Questions B

Student book page 4

1 **A** Input devices

B Processor and internal memory devices

C Output devices

D Secondary storage devices

2 **a** **i** Read Only Memory

ii Random Access Memory

b Contents are lost when the computer is turned off **RAM**

Contents are not lost when the computer is turned off **ROM**

Stores the programs needed to start up the computer **ROM**

Stores application programs and data when they are being used **RAM**

3 a One mark each for two of the following:

Applications will run faster.

More applications can be opened and run at the same time.

Users are able to move more quickly between applications.

b Two marks for a correct use for ROM and two marks each for a correct use for RAM.

ROM: Stores the boot program (1) which is the program needed to start up the computer (1).

RAM: Stores the systems software/operating system/applications software (1) along with the user's files (1).

Questions C

Student book page 6

1 a Any three from the following (one mark each):

Windows

Icons

Menus/Pull-down menus

Pointers

Online help/Office assistants

b One mark for one of the following:

Menu driven interface

Command line interface

Voice driven interface

Touch screen interface

2 a Two marks for two points similar to the following:

Programs used to control the hardware directly

Manages the system resources

b One mark each for three of the following:

Handles the inputs and outputs – controls the operation of input and output devices such as the keyboard, mouse, printer, screen, etc.

Recognises hardware attached to the computer – recognises that a device such as a pen drive has been attached and loads the software needed to control it.

Supervises the running of other programs – it provides a way for the applications software such as word-processing software to work with the hardware.

Handles the storage of data – decides where to store data in the memory and allows the user to create folders and sub-folders, etc.

Maximises the use of computer memory – decides where in memory the program instructions are placed.

Handles the interrupts and decides what action to take – a paper jam will stop the printer and alert the user with a message on the screen.

3 a One mark each for two user interfaces:

Graphical user interface

Command line interface

Touch screen interface

Voice driven interface

b **Benefits of a GUI:**

Considered to be more user friendly compared to a CLI

No commands to remember

Easier to find programs that are running by opening separate windows

Easier to pass data from one program to another

Drawbacks of a GUI:

Can be faster to type in commands rather than move the mouse and click

Needs a lot of memory for its operation

GUI needs a lot of hard disk space for its storage

Needs a powerful processor to use it

Benefits of a CLI:

CLI can be faster to use as you only have to type in a short command

Does not need as much memory compared to a GUI

Does not need as much hard disk space when being used

You do not need the latest processor to run a CLI

Drawbacks of a CLI:

Hard to learn as there are lots of commands to remember

Commands have a certain syntax which must be used so you need to be very precise

Benefits of a touch screen interface:

Very little training is needed to use the software

You do not need a flat surface on which to move a mouse

Drawbacks of a touch screen interface:

Dirty screens can make the screen hard to read

If lots of people use them then they can pass on germs

Benefits of a voice driven interface:

Safer to give verbal commands such as when driving

Can issue commands in the same way humans communicate with each other

Drawbacks of a voice driven interface:

Background noise can confuse the software

Commands have to be spoken precisely

Revision questions

Student book page 10

1 One mark each for:

Hardware – the physical components of a computer system (e.g. keyboard, mouse, printer, etc.)

Software – the set of instructions/programs that allows the hardware to do a useful task

2 a One mark for:

Processes the raw data by performing searching, sorting, calculating and decision making

b One mark for:

Stores program instructions and data that are needed immediately by the processor

c One mark for:

Used to hold programs and data that are not needed instantly by the computer

Used for long-term storage of programs and data

Used for backup copies in case the original data is damaged or lost

3 a One mark each for two input devices such as:

Keyboard

Mouse

Touch screen

Microphone

Barcode reader

etc.

b One mark for two output devices such as:

Printer

Screen/Monitor

Loudspeaker

etc.

c One mark for two backing storage devices such as:

Magnetic hard drive

Flash memory/Pen drive

CD drive

DVD drive

etc.

4 a One mark for each point to a maximum of three marks:

Desktop much larger in size or laptop much smaller

Desktop designed to be used in one place or laptop is portable

Desktop has full-sized screen/keyboard

Laptop is much lighter compared to a desktop

Laptop is sometimes operated by battery away from the mains power supply

b One mark for each point to a maximum of two marks:

Smaller than a laptop

Usually less memory

Mainly aimed at accessing the internet

Does not usually have a CD/DVD drive to reduce weight

5 One mark for one of the following:

Easier to use whilst standing up

Lighter so easier to transport

6 a One mark for a difference such as:

Main memory is internal hardware whereas backing storage is external hardware.

Backing storage is removable.

Main memory usually offers faster retrieval compared to backing storage.

b One mark for an answer similar to the following:

Data currently being processed

Current program instructions

Programs and data (i.e. stored on hard disk)

c One mark for an answer similar to the following:

Data and programs for later use

Backups which need to be stored off-site

Programs which need to be installed

7 a One mark for:

An internal hardware device is situated within the computer casing whereas an external hardware device is outside

b One mark each for two examples of internal hardware devices such as:

Motherboard

RAM

ROM

Video card

Sound card

Network interface card

Internal hard disk drive

One mark each for two examples of external hardware devices such as:

Monitors/Screens

Keyboard

Mouse/Mice

External hard disk drive

Memory stick

Scanner

Speaker

Microphone

8 a One mark each for Random Access Memory and Read-only Memory.

b One mark for each difference:

ROM – the contents remain when the power is removed.

RAM – the contents are lost when the power is removed.

ROM – stores the programs and instructions needed to start up the computer.

RAM – stores the programs and data currently being used.

9 One mark for the name of the emerging technology, two marks for a description of what the technology is and two marks for explaining how it is likely to change lives.

This is just one of the many answers you could have:

Vision enhancement

Used to enhance vision to make it easier to see

Uses special sensors (which are usually special cameras) that detect information from images outside the visible spectrum

This information is then put together with the ordinary image to make it clearer

People with low vision can use vision enhancement to enable them to see using their remaining sight

10 a One mark for:

Using ICT and a unique property of the human body (fingerprints, face, iris and retina) to identify a person

b One mark each for two of the following:

Iris pattern

Retina pattern

Face measurements

Fingerprints

c Two marks for explanation of the uses:

Iris pattern – uses the unique pattern on the iris to identify a person to allow them access to a room

Retina pattern – uses the unique pattern on the back of the eye (i.e. the retina) to allow a person access

Face measurements – uses measurements from a CCTV camera to make a match with the measurements stored in a passport to allow a person entry into a country or not

Fingerprints – uses the unique pattern on a fingerprint to identify a pupil in a registration system in a school. The pupil puts their finger into a reader and the system identifies them

Test yourself

Student book page 11

A software

B hardware

C CPU information

D software

E applications

F desktop

G input

H output

I backing storage

J RAM

K ROM

L ROM

M RAM

N gesture

O augmented

Exam-style questions

Student book page 12

1 One mark for each of the following:

Renaming a file

Deciding where to store data on a hard disk drive

Loading a file from the disk drive

2 a One mark for each one such as:

To provide a user interface (i.e. a way for the user to interact with the computer)

To control the system resources and the processing

To handle outputs

To maximise the use of computer memory

To handle interrupts and decide what action to take

b One mark for an answer such as:

Used to supply the instructions to the computer to instruct it how to use the attached device

3

	Description	Name
A	Deals with errors that occur when the computer is working on tasks	Operating system
B	Software needed when a new piece of hardware is attached to the computer	Device driver
C	Scans the hard disk drive to detect and remove viruses	Utility

4

	True	False
Computer programs are examples of software.	√	
Creating a new folder would be performed by a device driver.		√
A compiler is an example of an operating system.		√
Word-processing software is an example of applications software.	√	

5 One mark for each task:

a Transferring data to a printer

b Allocating storage space on a disk

e Accepting keyboard input

6 One mark for each of three functions such as:

Handles inputs and outputs

Supervises the running of other software

Handles the storage of data

Maximises the use of computer memory

Handles the interrupts and decides what action to take

7 One mark for each of four differences such as:

ROM – the contents remain when the power is removed

RAM – the contents are lost when the power is removed

ROM – stores the programs and instructions needed to start up the computer

RAM – stores the programs and data currently being used

8 One mark each:

a Software , **b** Input, **c** Output, **d** ROM, **e** RAM.

9 **a** One mark each for two advantages such as:

Easier to use standing up

Lighter and so more portable

Can be used to take photographs

b One mark each for two disadvantages such as:

Usually only an on-screen keyboard is provided, which makes it hard to type long documents

No CD/DVD drive so films and music have to be downloaded

Small screen makes it more difficult for people with poor eyesight to use

c One mark for each of three features such as:

Windows

Icons

Menus/Pull-down menus

Pointers

Online help/Office assistants

10 One mark each for two tasks such as:

Vacuuming carpets in a house

Assembling components in a factory

Paint spraying in a car factory

Welding panels in a car factory

11 One mark for each correct tick.

Robots are more intelligent than humans.	
Robots are cheap to buy and maintain.	
Robots can work 24 hours a day.	√
Robots always assemble the parts correctly.	√
Robots need to be programmed to perform a task.	
It is cheaper as robots are not paid wages.	√

12 One mark each for six differences such as:

With a CLI you have to type in the instructions.

With a GUI you can just click on an icon.

There is a lot more to learn in order to use a CLI.

With a CLI the instructions must be entered precisely (e.g. in a certain order).

A GUI uses Windows, Icons, Menus and Pointers to allow users to accomplish tasks.

Using a CLI to run a program, you have to remember the path where the program file is located.

13 One mark each for four points similar to the following:

Stand-alone computers: are not connected to a network; they do not share resources or files with other computers; all the programs and data files needed for the applications are stored locally (i.e. on one of the drives or memory in the computer itself).

Networked computers: are linked to a network or other computers; are able to share files, an internet connection and devices such as printers and scanners; programs are stored on the internet (i.e. cloud storage) rather than locally on the computer.

14 One mark each for three advantages such as:

A CLI uses a series of commands which need to be memorised, which can be difficult.

Using a keyboard with a CLI can give rise to health problems when using a keyboard and mouse.

Using a GUI is faster as you use your fingers or a stylus rather than a keyboard.

GUIs make use of scrolling, pinching and expanding where CLIs have none of these features.

Using a CLI you type in commands in full, but with a GUI you just click on an icon.

15 One mark each for four internal devices and one mark each for four external devices:

Internal hardware devices

Motherboard

RAM

ROM

Video card

Sound card

Internal hard disk drive

External hardware devices

Monitors/screens

Keyboard and mouse

External hardware devices

Printers

Scanners

Speakers

Microphones

16 One mark for each correctly placed tick:

	Ram	Rom
Can have data written to or read from it	√	
Retains data when the power is lost		√
Is temporary storage for programs and data	√	
Is non-volatile		√

17 a Technology that superimposes computer-generated images on the user's views of the real word. A composite view is then produced.

b The mechanic can view the engine with all the parts labelled by the computer.

The mechanic is taken through the steps as they look at the actual engine of the car make and model they are working on.

They do not need to refer to an online or paper-based manual.

They can work on unfamiliar engines with the help given.

Worksheet 1.1: What is being shown here?

Teacher resource pack page 6

1 Desktop computer
2 Processor
3 Fixed hard disk
4 Mouse
5 Tablet
6 Scanner
7 Internal memory
8 Motherboard
9 Laptop computer
10 Sound card

Worksheet 1.2: Hardware or software?

Teacher resource pack page 9

	Name of item	Hardware	Software
1	Processor	√	
2	Operating system		√
3	Fixed hard disk	√	
4	Memory chips (RAM and ROM)	√	
5	Keyboard	√	
6	Mouse	√	
7	Word processor		√
8	Search engine		√
9	Speakers	√	
10	Microphone	√	
11	DVD drive	√	
12	Blank DVD	√	
13	Database		√
14	Spreadsheet		√
15	Barcode reader	√	
16	Printer	√	
17	Web browser		√
18	Removable hard disk	√	
19	Wireless router	√	
20	Digital camera	√	

Input and output devices

This worksheet can be best used following study of input and output devices in Chapter 2 of the Student Book.

Worksheet 2.1

Input and output crossword

Complete the crossword using the clues on the next page.

Worksheet 2.1 (continued)

Across

2. Useful for capturing old photographs so they can be stored on a computer.
3. You get a magnetic one of these on a credit card.
6. Almost every computer comes with one of these input devices.
9. One of these is useful for playing games.
10. You enter data by speaking into one of these.

Down

1. This kind of tablet is an input device often used for freehand drawings.
4. You can see who you are chatting to with one of these.
5. Temperature data can come from these.
7. Very popular input device which can be wired or wireless.
8. These characters can be read by a scanner and special software.

This worksheet can be best used following study of input and output devices in Chapter 2 of the Student Book.

Worksheet 2.2

Can you name the input or output devices shown?

Give the name of the input or output device shown.

1

Name:

2

Name:

3

Name:

4

Name:

Worksheet 2.2 (continued)

5

Name:

6

Name:

7

Name:

8

Name:

Worksheet 2.2 (continued)

9

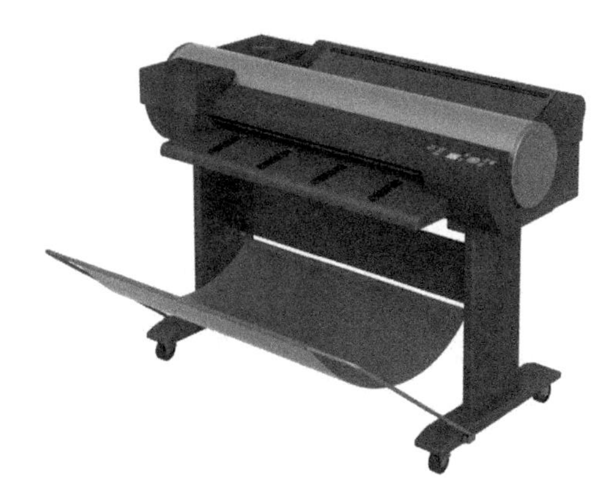

Name:

10

Name:

Topic 2 answers

Questions A

Student book page 19

1 a One mark for each of the following:
Graphics tablet
Mouse
Microphone
Touch screen
Digital still camera
Webcam

b One mark each for two of:
Colour laser printer
Speakers
Touch screen
LCD screen

2 a One mark for a definition similar to the following:
Hardware devices used for the entry of instructions or data into the computer for processing

b One mark each for two suitable answers such as:
Keyboard
Mouse
Touch pad
Touch screen

c One mark for touch pad

3 One mark for each correct answer:
Keyboard
Touch pad
Webcam
Touch screen

4 One mark each for two items:
Webcam
Touch screen
Temperature sensor

5 One mark for each of two points such as:
There is no additional item to have to carry.
They can be used when there is no flat surface to use a mouse.

6 One mark for each correct answer.

Input device	Use
Keyboard	Entering text when writing a book
Remote control	Operating a television
Touch screen	Used to make selections on tablets and some smartphones
Numeric keypad	Used to enter a PIN when making a purchase
Pressure sensor	Used when checking the depth of water in a container
Temperature sensor	Used as the input for an air conditioning unit to keep the temperature of a room constant
Scanner	For inputting a hand-drawn drawing into the computer

Questions B

Student book page 22

1 One mark for each correct answer.
a Optical mark reader
b Optical character reader
c Magnetic stripe reader
d Chip and PIN readers
e Magnetic ink character reader

2 One mark for each answer:
a Magnetic stripe reader
b Numeric keypad
c Barcode reader
d Touch screen

3 a One mark for each of three points such as:
Obtains data stored on a tag (a small chip) using radio signals
The reading device and tag do not have to come into contact with each other
Data on the tag can be read from a distance
RFID is a wireless system

b One mark for another example such as:
Cattle can be tagged so the milking system can identify which cow is being milked and information about yield, etc., can be stored
Used for season tickets to car parks
Used in libraries as a replacement for barcodes

c One mark for each of two advantages such as:
Tags can be read at a distance, so you could have a tag on you which could be read without getting it out of your pocket or bag.
You can store a lot of data on the tags.

4 a iii
b ii
c iv
d v
e vi
f i

Questions C

Student book page 28

1 One mark for each of five output devices:

Buzzer

Speakers

Motor

Multimedia projector

Touch screen

2

Output device	Use
Multimedia projector	Used to make presentations to a large audience
Buzzer	Used as an alert on smartphones
Light	Used as a warning on a car to show it is low on fuel
Wide format printer	Used for outputting large posters, maps and plans
Dot matrix printer	Used for producing multi-part invoices
CRT monitor	A large monitor used by older computers
TFT/LCD monitor	A thin lightweight monitor

3 One mark for each of three differences such as:

Inkjet printers are generally smaller in size compared to laser printers

Laser printers use toner cartridges whereas inkjet printers use ink cartridges

Laser printers have a lower cost per page and are therefore cheaper to run if lots of pages need to be printed

Faster printing speed compared to an inkjet printer

Laser printers are more expensive to purchase

4 One application such as:

Use on a smartphone to output information on a screen

Use on laptop to provide a user interface that is easy to use

5 a One mark for each point to a maximum of six marks:

Dot matrix printers can be used to print on multi-part stationery

Dot matrix printers are impact printers and are therefore noisy

Dot matrix printers cannot properly print graphics

Laser printers are more expensive, especially for colour

Inkjet printers can produce high quality colour images cheaply

Laser printers are much faster

Laser printers are cheaper to run if lots of copies are printed regularly

If you are only printing in black and white then a laser printer would be best

For home use where relatively few copies are printed and you also need to print in colour, then an inkjet printer would be best

Inkjet printers can smudge the ink

b It is very unlikely a home user would ever purchase a dot matrix printer so marks are only awarded for a laser or inkjet printer

An answer for an inkjet printer

Cheap to purchase but expensive to run, so ideal for low volume work

A cheap way of printing in colour (colour lasers are expensive)

An answer for a laser printer

More expensive to buy but cheaper to run

Faster printouts

Do not need to change the toner as often as inkjet cartridges

Revision questions

Student book page 28

1 a One mark for each correct output device:

LCD monitor

Laser printer

Speakers

b One mark each for two output devices such as:

Motor

Plotter

Multimedia projector

Robot arm

Buzzer

c One mark for an input device such as:

Magnetic stripe reader

Optical character reader

Optical mark reader

Barcode reader

Remote control

Tracker ball

Joystick

Scanner

2 a i One mark for each use to a maximum of two marks:

Making selections

Bring up a menu of items using right click

Issuing a command

Dragging and dropping

etc.

ii One mark for each use to a maximum of two marks:

Recording live music

Dictating text using voice recognition

Using voicemail

Issuing a command using voice recognition

Recording speech/narration to add to a website or presentation

iii One mark for each use to a maximum of two marks:

Taking digital still photographs

Taking digital video

Using as a webcam

Using to produce frames for animation

b One mark for the name of each output device and one mark for the use. Examples include:

Printer to produce a hard copy

Screen to display web pages

Plotter to produce a map or plan on paper

Speakers to listen to music

etc.

3 One mark for each correct answer (i.e. total of 10 marks).

Application	Most suitable output device
Alerting the user that an error has occurred by making a beep	Loudspeaker/speaker
Printing a poster in colour	Inkjet printer/Laser printer
Listening to a radio station using the internet	Loudspeaker/speaker/headphones
Producing a large plan of a house	Plotter/Graph plotter/Wide format printer
Producing a hard copy of a spreadsheet	Printer (any type)
Producing a colour picture on paper taken with a digital camera	Inkjet printer/Colour laser printer
Producing a series of invoices with several copies that can be sent to different departments	Dot matrix printer
Producing a warning when a barcode is read incorrectly	Loudspeaker/speaker
Listening to messages from a voicemail system	Loudspeaker/speaker
Displaying the results of a quick search on the availability of a holiday	Screen/Monitor/VDU

4 **a** One mark for each point allocated in the following way:

Items/Icons/Menus appear on the screen

You touch the item on the screen to make a selection

b One mark for an advantage such as:

They can be easily used whilst standing up.

They are very simple to use as you just touch the item you want.

There is no complicated keyboard to use.

5 **a** Laser printer

b Inkjet printer

c Inkjet printer

d Inkjet printer

e Laser printer

f Inkjet printer

g 3D printer

Test yourself

Student book page 29

A input

B keyboard

C mouse

D touch pad

E joysticks

F microphone

G scanner

H optical character recognition

I digital

J RFID

K sensors

L output

M laser

N inkjet

O touch

P actuator

Q QR

Exam-style questions

Student book page 30

1 One mark each for the following ringed items:

Wide format printer

Multimedia projector

2 One mark each for each correct pairing:

Scanner – For digitising an old photograph so it can be put on a website

Touch screen – For inputting selections when buying a train ticket

Chip reader – Reading information on a credit/debit card

Microphone – For recording narration to be used with a presentation

3 One mark for each correct answer:

a Dot matrix

b Wide format printers

c Touch screens

d Inkjet

4 One mark for each of the following:

Dot matrix printer advantages

Can be used with continuous stationery

Can be used to print multi-part stationery/carbon copies

Cheaper to run compared to inkjet and laser printers

Can print through a payslip cover so that pay details are kept confidential

Dot matrix printer disadvantages

More expensive to buy

Very noisy

Low quality printouts can make the text harder to read

Relatively slow

Laser printer advantages

Very fast output

Relatively quiet compared to inkjet and dot matrix printers

No wet pages that smudge like the inkjet printer

Supplies last longer

Laser printer disadvantages

More expensive running costs than a dot matrix printer

More expensive to buy initially than an inkjet printer

Size as most laser printers are larger than inkjet printers

Advantages of inkjet printers

Quieter than a dot matrix printer

Cheaper to purchase initially

Disadvantages of inkjet printers

Inkjet cartridges do not last long

The ink on the paper can smudge

Hard to print a sealed secured payslip

Inkjet cartridges are expensive so this makes them expensive to run

5 One mark each for:

A = Magnetic stripe reader

B = RFID reader

C = Scanner

D = Trackerball

E = QR scanner

6 a One mark for each one of the following: Pressure sensor, Touch screen, Mouse, RFID reader, Magnetic ink character reader (MICR), Barcode reader and Light sensor.

b One mark for each one of the following: Touch screen, Wide format printer, Laser printer, Motor and Light

c One mark each:

i Pressure sensor

ii Wide format printer

iii Barcode reader

iv Light sensor

v Motor

7 a One mark for each of two points:

An actuator responds to control signals which it receives from a computer or microprocessor. It provides motion to move something, such as close a valve.

b One mark each for two output devices:

Light

Heater

Motor

Buzzer

Screen/Monitor/LCD display/LED display

Printer

Graph plotter

8 a Two marks for:

Optical Mark Recognition/Reader

Optical Character Recognition/Reader

b One mark for each comparison up to a maximum of six marks.

Using OCR and OMR is faster than entering the data using a keyboard

OMR is limited to reading marks on paper forms such as exam answers or school registers.

OCR can be used to identify car registration plates at ports and car parks.

OCR can be used to identify car registration plates when cars are caught speeding, jumping red lights or not having car tax.

Errors are more likely when OCR is used.

You need pre-printed stationery with OMR.

OCR is used in tablets to recognise handwriting on the touch screen which can be turned into text.

Keyboard entry is more accurate than OCR but less accurate than OMR.

No extra input device needs to be purchased as all computers come with keyboards.

9 One mark each for two advantages and two disadvantages such as:

Advantages:

Can print on paper larger than A4 so is ideal for printing maps, scale drawings, posters, etc.

Do not need to use the services of professional print ships which can be expensive.

Disadvantages:

Expensive especially if only used occasionally.

Wide format printers are quite large which can be a problem in small offices where space is limited.

As the paper size is larger, the ink cartridges will not last long and they are expensive to replace.

10 a One mark for each of two points similar to the following:

A 3D design is produced on the screen which can then be printed in 3D.

Prints by building up successive layers of material such as plastic, glass or ceramic.

A 3D model or product can then be produced.

b One mark for each of two uses similar to the following:

Dentistry for the production of crowns, implants and false teeth.

Hearing aids that fit ears perfectly.

Production of components which can then be assembled to produce a final product.

Prosthetic limbs can be manufactures which fit the patient perfectly.

Worksheet 2.1: Input and output crossword

Teacher resource pack page 17

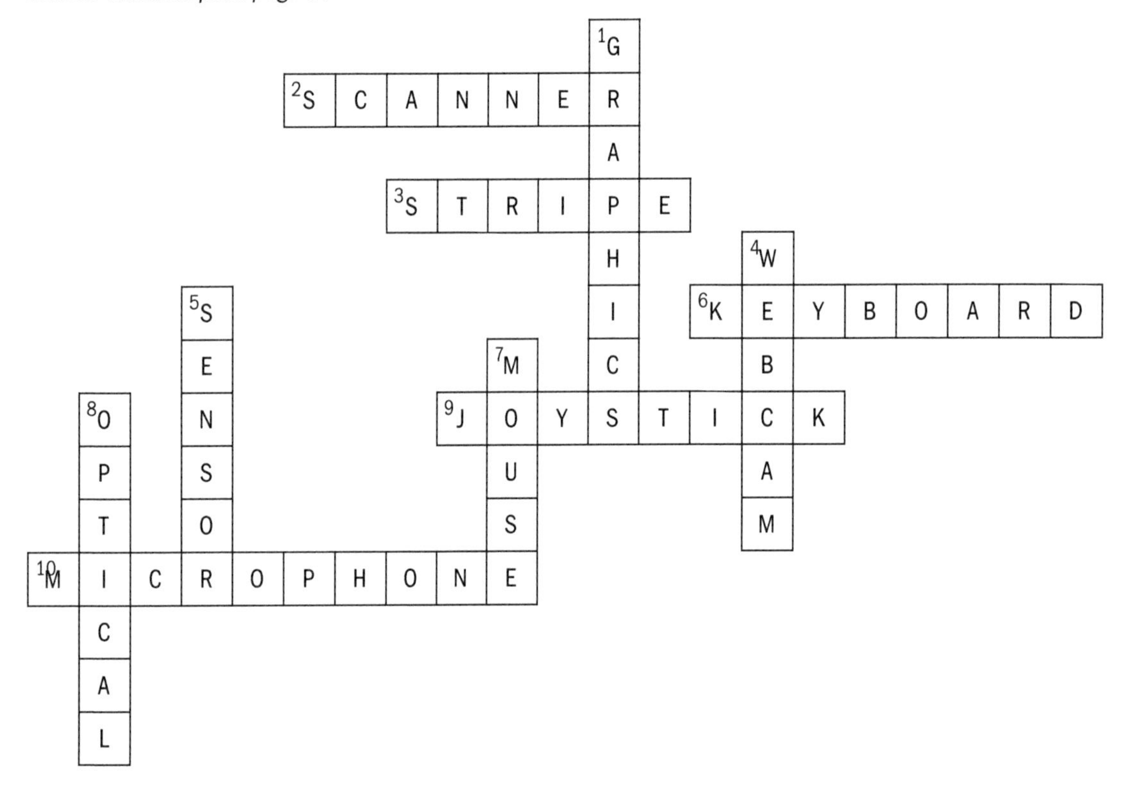

Worksheet 2.2: Can you name the input or output devices shown?

Teacher resource pack page 19

1. Mouse
2. Speakers/loudspeakers
3. Printer
4. QR scanner on mobile phone
5. Digital camera
6. Microphone
7. webcam
8. Touch screen
9. Plotter
10. Remote control

Storage devices and media

This worksheet can be best used following study of backing storage devices and media in Chapter 3 on page 31 of the Student Book.

Worksheet 3.1

The differences between the two types of memory ROM and RAM

You have to decide whether each of the following statements refers to ROM or RAM by placing a tick in the relevant columns.

	Statement	ROM	RAM
1	Stands for Read-only Memory		
2	Stands for Random Access Memory		
3	Loses its contents when the power is switched off		
4	Contents remain when the power is switched off		
5	Classed as volatile memory		
6	Classed as non-volatile memory		
7	Is read/write		
8	Is read only		
9	The user is able to alter its contents		
10	Used to hold the instructions needed to start the computer up		

This worksheet can be best used following study of backing storage devices and media in Chapter 3 of the Student Book.

Worksheet 3.2

Can you name the storage device/media shown?

Give the name of the storage device/media shown.

1

Name:

____

2

Name:

____

3

Name:

____

Worksheet 3.2 (continued)

4

Name:

5

Name:

Topic 3 answers

Questions A

Student book page 35

1 One mark for each of the following:

Hard drive

CD-RW drive

Pen drive

2 a One mark for Digital Versatile Disk Recordable

b One mark for Digital Versatile Disk Read/Write

3 a One mark for an answer similar to the following:

A copy of original programs and data kept in case the original data is damaged or lost

b So that only a small amount of data would be lost should the original data or programs be damaged or lost

c One mark for the name and two marks for two points explaining its suitability

Portable hard disk

Can be stored in a different place to the original data

Data can be stored on the device at high speed

Test yourself

Student book page 35

A backups

B immediately

C backing

D programs

E hard

F cartridges

G DVD

H solid

I cloud

Revision questions

Student book page 36

1 a i One mark for each of the following to a maximum of two marks:

Storing applications programs

Storing the operating system software

Storing user data

ii One mark for each of the following to a maximum of two marks:

For copying downloaded music so it can be used on a CD player

For distributing programs

To hold music

b One mark each for two ways such as:

High capacities mean users are not restricted with how much data can be held

Possible to make them very small so the whole piece of equipment can be made small

They are light to make them more portable

2 a One mark for a difference such as:

Main internal memory is stored in a chip

Backing storage holds a lot more data

Main internal memory offers faster retrieval

b One mark for an answer similar to the following:

Data currently being processed

Current program instructions

c One mark for an answer similar to the following:

Data which needs to be stored permanently

Programs which need to be installed

3 One mark for each use and two marks for the explanation.

a Used for the storage of digital photographs in digital cameras because the cards have a high capacity and are small and light

b Used for storage of programs as most computers are equipped with CD drives capable of reading the programs so that they can be installed

c Used for the storage of programs and data because of their very high storage capacity and the high speed at which they read and write data

d Used for the storage of data and ideal for the transfer of data between computers, for example for transferring data between school and home

Exam-style questions

Student book page 37

1 a One mark for each of the following: flash memory card, memory stick

b One mark for: magnetic tape

c One mark for: CD-RW

d One mark for each of the following: portable hard disk, magnetic tape

2 One mark each for three reasons:

Pen drives have a higher storage capacity.

Pen drives are more portable.

They offer faster access to data.

They are more robust/CDs are easily scratched.

They can be more secure as they can be protected using biometric methods such as fingerprinting.

No additional hardware is needed as pen drives simply slot into a USB port.

3 A = CD-RW
   B = Pen drive
   C = Magnetic tape
   D = Magnetic disk
4 One mark each for two of the following:
   Portable hard disks have a higher storage capacity.
   Their transfer rate is higher meaning that less time is spent transferring the files.
   They are larger in size which means they are less likely to be lost or stolen.
5 One mark for each of two advantages:
   Takes less time to access data/lower access time
   Takes less time to transfer data/greater rate of transfer of data
   Can store more data
6 One mark for each of three advantages and one mark for each of three disadvantages.

   Advantages

   You can access files from any device connected to the internet.

   You no longer need to use portable storage that can easily be damaged or lost.

   Data can be shared across many users which is useful if several people are working on the same project.

   You do not need to worry about backup as the company providing cloud storage does this for you.

   Disadvantages

   You cannot access the files without internet access.

   There is usually a limited amount of free storage but if you require more, you need to pay a subscription.

   Stored data may not be secure.

   The organisation providing the cloud storage could go out of business causing loss of your data.

   Does not work well with low-speed internet connections.
7 One mark for a use and a reason × 2.
   Used to distribute software and games
   Optical disks are cheap to produce and post
   Making backups of data
   Most desktops come with the drives and this is cheaper than purchasing additional hardware such as a tape drive

Worksheet 3.1: The differences between the two types of memory ROM and RAM

Teacher resource pack page 27

	Statement	ROM	RAM
1	Stands for Read-only Memory	√	
2	Stands for Random Access Memory		√
3	Loses its contents when the power is switched off		√
4	Contents remain when the power is switched off	√	
5	Classed as volatile memory		√
6	Classed as non-volatile memory	√	
7	Is read/write		√
8	Is read only	√	
9	The user is able to alter its contents		√
10	Used to hold the instructions needed to start the computer up	√	

Worksheet 3.2: Can you name the storage device/media shown?

Teacher resource pack page 28

1 Magnetic hard drive/hard drive
2 Blu-ray disc
3 Memory stick/pen drive/USB drive/flash memory
4 Memory card
5 Memory chips/RAM or ROM/main memory

Networks and the effects of using them

This worksheet can be best used following study of networks and the effects of using them in Chapter 4 of the Student Book.

Worksheet 4.1

Networks wordsearch

Answer the questions below to complete the list of words. Three have been done for you.
Then find the ten words in the wordsearch on the next page. The words could be written backwards, forwards or diagonally.

1. Method of keeping data private. E_ _ _ _ _ _ _ _N
2. People who gain illegal access to a computer. HACKERS
3. A copy of important files and information. B_ _ _U_
4. What encryption does to the data. S_ _ _ _ _ _ _S
5. A data _________ law requires that personal data is kept secure. P_ _ _ _ _ _ _ _N
6. An authentication technique making use of a property of the human body. BIOMETRIC
7. The largest network. I_ _ _ _ _ _T
8. A network used inside an organisation. I_ _ _ _ _ _T
9. Device for joining networks. R_ _ _ _R
10. Type of signal used to send information. RADIO

Worksheet 4.1 (continued)

N	O	P	K	U	H	L	T	Z	S	E	J	S	W	S
N	O	P	U	H	L	E	Q	E	T	N	U	G	N	I
N	Z	I	U	K	N	N	L	L	D	C	W	Q	E	C
W	R	H	T	A	C	B	H	J	F	R	C	V	J	T
D	V	E	R	C	M	A	E	E	I	Y	I	X	M	H
T	T	T	T	A	E	Y	B	H	C	P	Y	Y	R	U
L	N	Q	R	U	R	T	B	R	G	T	G	L	B	P
I	A	C	Z	H	O	A	O	T	H	I	L	L	U	T
L	S	H	W	E	R	R	D	R	K	O	L	B	I	R
T	E	N	R	E	T	N	I	I	P	N	C	W	Z	C
H	E	K	O	O	N	F	E	Y	O	W	Y	S	M	C
C	F	H	X	B	B	O	U	L	D	B	O	M	E	S
P	W	R	H	A	C	K	E	R	S	J	D	U	S	H
C	I	R	T	E	M	O	I	B	U	D	D	C	L	A
A	U	I	Q	N	L	I	F	P	I	N	D	J	L	D

Topic 4 answers

Questions A

Student book page 41

1 Router/Wireless router

2 Two marks outlining a difference.

Hub - does not manage any network traffic through it

Data packets are transmitted to all the other ports

Switch - manages network traffic

Inspects the packages of data so they are only sent to the computer/device they are intended for

3 a One mark for each name in a suitable pair of devices such as:

Keyboard and computer

Mouse and computer

Mobile phone and computer

Camera and computer

Computer and printer

etc.

b One mark for an advantage such as:

No direct connection is needed so it is easier

No need to hunt for a cable to make the connection

c One mark for a disadvantage such as:

Bluetooth only has a short range which limits its use

There is a danger of hackers accessing the system

4 One mark for each advantage to a maximum of two marks:

No wires to sink/conceal

Can work anywhere in the office or even close to the office outside

Easier to keep the offices clean

Fewer trailing wires to trip over

5 a One mark for a reason such as:

Lower installation costs as there are no network wires to buy and install

Can work anywhere in the building

b One mark for: So that several/many computers can share a single connection to the internet

6 One mark for: They may be worried that hackers may gain access to the network.

Questions B

Student book page 43

1 One mark for each benefit to a maximum of two marks.

You can send and receive email from anyone on the LAN.

You can share the same data files.

Software can be updated centrally.

Hardware devices such as printers and scanners can be shared.

2 One mark for any of the following.

LAN (local area network)	WAN (wide area network)
Confined to a small area	Cover a wide geographical area (e.g. between cities, countries and even continents)
Usually located in a single building	In lots of different buildings and cities, countries, etc.
Uses cable, wireless, infra-red and microwave links which are usually owned by the organisation	Uses more expensive telecommunication links that are supplied by telecommunication companies (e.g. satellite links)
Cheaper to build as equipment is owned by the organisation	Expensive to build as sophisticated communication systems are used
Slower speed connections	High speed connections
Cheaper to run as less expertise is needed	Expensive to run as highly qualified and expensive staff are needed to keep network running

3 One mark each for two advantages and two disadvantages.

Advantages

- You can share hardware - you share printers, scanners and the equipment such as modems and routers used to provide an internet connection.
- Software can be installed in one place - you do not need to install software on each computer. This makes it faster to install and easier to maintain. If the software needs to be upgraded, then this is much easier if only one copy is used.
- Work can be backed up centrally by the network manager, which means users do not have to back up their own work. The network manager will make sure that the work is backed up.
- Passwords make sure that other people cannot access your work unless you want them to
- Speed - it is very quick to copy and transfer files.
- Cost - network versions of software can be bought and these are much cheaper than buying a copy for each stand-alone computer.
- Email facilities - any user of the network will be able to communicate using electronic mail. This will be much more efficient compared to paper-based documents such as memos, etc.
- Access to a central store of data - users will have access to centrally stored data.

Disadvantages

- A network manager will need to be employed - this can be quite expensive.
- Security problems - a virus could get onto the system and cause problems or hackers may gain access to the data on the network.

- Breakdown problems – if the network breaks down, users will not have access to the important information held.
- Expensive – a server and cables and/or other communication devices will be needed. The installation costs of a network are also high.

4 One mark for each of two differences such as:

An intranet is a private network used within an organisation that makes use of internet technology for sharing internal information.

The internet is a huge network of networks which anyone can access.

The information on an intranet is confined to information related to a particular company or organisation.

The information on the internet is about every subject imaginable.

Intranet access is restricted to certain groups of people such as the staff working in an organisation or their trading partners.

5 One mark for each point to a maximum of two marks.

Web browser software is a program that allows web pages stored on the internet to be viewed.

Web browsers read the instructions on how to display the items on a web page which are written in a form called HTML (Hypertext Markup Language).

6 **a** One mark for:

A wired LAN uses cables to transfer data between computers and other devices on the network, whereas a WLAN uses radio signals to transfer the data.

b One mark each for two advantages such as:

No wires to sink/conceal

Can work anywhere in the office or even close to the office outside

Easier to keep the offices clean

Fewer trailing wires to trip over

One mark each for two disadvantages such as:

It is easier for wireless signals to be hacked into

Data transfer speeds are lower compared to using wires

Questions C

Student book page 48

1 One mark for each answer:

a True

b False

c True

d True

e False

f True

2 One mark for each point up to a maximum of four marks:

A weak password is more likely to be guessed by a hacker.

A weak password would be the name of your pet or football team, etc.

Weak passwords are words or names.

Weak passwords are short.

Strong passwords are not likely to be guessed.

Strong passwords are not words or names.

Strong passwords consist of upper and lower case letters, numbers and symbols.

3 **a** One mark each for two of the following:

Medical details

Credit history

Criminal record

Religion

Political beliefs

b Two marks for a point such as:

Medical details could be wrong so you could get the wrong treatment.

The details could say incorrectly that you had a criminal record which could mean you are refused a job.

4 **a** One mark for each item such as:

Medical details

Religious beliefs

Exam grades

b One mark for each of two rights such as:

The right to see the personal data held about them

The right to have the information corrected if it is wrong

The right to ensure that the data is kept secure and up-to-date

c Two points for an answer such as:

The exam results could be wrong, meaning they might not get a place at university.

5 One mark for each of three data protection principles such as:

Data should be processed fairly and lawfully.

Personal data should only be obtained for one specified purpose.

Personal data collected should not be excessive.

Personal data should be accurate and kept up-to-date.

Personal data should not be kept for longer than is necessary.

Personal data should be processed in accordance with the rights of the person the data is about.

Steps should be taken to protect the data from unauthorised access.

Personal data should not be transferred to a country that does not have adequate data protection laws.

6 a One mark for an answer similar to:

Using a property of the human body (fingerprint, retinal pattern, iris pattern, face measurements) to enable an ICT system to identify a person

b One mark for each description to a maximum of three marks:

Fingerprint – uses the unique pattern on fingertips to identify a person

Retinal pattern – uses the unique pattern on the retina to identify a person

Iris pattern – uses the unique pattern on the iris to identify a person

Face measurements – measures distances between certain points on the face to identify a person

Questions D

Student book page 50

1 a One mark for each point to a maximum of two marks.

ICT system that allows virtual face-to-face meetings to be conducted without the participants being in the same room or even the same geographical area

b One mark each for two benefits such as:

Less stress as employees do not have to experience delays at airports, accidents, road works, etc.

Improved family life, as less time spent away from home staying in hotels

They do not have to put in long working hours travelling to and from meetings

Saves money as business does not have to spend money on travelling expenses, hotel rooms, meals, etc.

Improved productivity of employees, as they are not wasting time travelling

Meetings can be called at very short notice without too much planning

Greener/more environmentally friendly as there are fewer people flying to meetings. This cuts down on carbon dioxide emissions

Roads will not be clogged up with traffic and this will cause less stress and reduce pollution

2 a One mark each for two reasons such as:

Other media such as radio, films and TV are policed so the internet should be.

There is free access to violence and pornography which is bad for society

The internet is used to promote illegal activity.

b One mark each for two reasons such as:

Free speech is a fundamental right.

It would be impossible to police properly and the resources would not be available.

You would need cooperation between all countries which is highly unlikely.

3 One mark each for two points such as:

Audio-conferencing involves conducting a meeting using just voice.

Video-conferencing allows two or more individuals situated in different places to talk to each other in real time and see each other at the same time.

Revision questions

Student book page 50

1 a i Local area network

ii Wide area network

b Two differences for two marks as outlined in this table.

LAN (local area network)	WAN (wide area network)
Confined to a small area	Cover a wide geographical area (e.g. between cities, countries and even continents)
Usually located in a single building	In lots of different buildings and cities, countries, etc.
Uses cable, wireless, infra-red and microwave links which are usually owned by the organisation	Uses more expensive telecommunication links that are supplied by telecommunication companies (e.g. satellite links)
Cheaper to build as equipment is owned by the organisation	Expensive to build as sophisticated communication systems are used
Slower speed connections	High speed connections
Cheaper to run as less expertise is needed	Expensive to run as highly qualified and expensive staff are needed to keep network running

c One mark for each advantage to a maximum of three marks.

You can share hardware – you share printers, scanners and the equipment such as modems and routers used to provide an internet connection.

Software can be installed in one place – you do not need to install software on each computer. This makes it faster to install and easier to maintain. If the software needs to be upgraded, then this is much easier if only one copy is used.

Work can be backed up centrally by the network manager, which means users do not have to back up their own work. The network manager will make sure that the work is backed up.

Passwords make sure that other people cannot access your work unless you want them to.

Speed – it is very quick to copy and transfer files.

Cost – network versions of software can be bought and these are much cheaper than buying a copy for each stand-alone computer.

Email facilities – any user of the network will be able to communicate using electronic mail. This will be much more efficient compared to paper-based documents such as memos, etc.

Access to a central store of data – users will have access to centrally stored data.

Backups are taken centrally – a network manager is responsible for taking regular backups. Users of stand-alone computers may forget to take backups.

d One mark for 'Encrypt/scramble the data'.

2 a One mark for credit/debit card.

b One mark for each point up to a maximum of two marks:

Their details may be hacked into.

The details can then be used to commit fraud.

c Two marks for an answer such as:

Details are encrypted which means that if they are hacked into they cannot be understood.

3 a One mark each for two points similar to the following:

Tells the network who is using the computer

Details can be added to the transaction log

Can tell who has accessed and altered files

b One mark each for two points similar to the following:

Ensures that the person who is using the user-ID is the correct person

Used to prevent unauthorised access

Used to prevent hackers accessing the network

c One mark each for two points similar to the following:

Scrambles the data

Only the correct recipient can view the data

Stored or passed through a network

So that if intercepted or stolen it cannot be understood

4 One mark each for an advantage/disadvantage up to a maximum of four marks:

Advantages:

Can work anywhere, provided you have a wireless signal anywhere in the building

Fewer/no trailing wires to trip over

It is easier to keep a working area clean if there are not as many wires in the way

No network wires so no cost associated with sinking them

Disadvantages:

The danger of hackers reading messages

There are areas where you cannot get a wireless network

There is some evidence that there may be a danger to your health

Limited signal range

5 a One mark each for two advantages:

Less stress as employees do not have to experience delays at airports, accidents, road works, etc.

Improved family life, as less time spent away from home staying in hotels

They do not have to put in long working hours travelling to and from meetings

Saves money as business does not have to spend money on travelling expenses, hotel rooms, meals, etc.

Improved productivity of employees, as they are not wasting time travelling

Meetings can be called at very short notice without too much planning

Greener as there are fewer people flying to meetings. This cuts down on carbon dioxide emissions

Roads will not be clogged up with traffic and this will cause less stress and reduce pollution

b One mark each for two disadvantages:

The cost of the equipment, as specialist video-conferencing equipment is expensive

Poor image and sound quality

People can feel very self-conscious when using video-conferencing and may fail to come across well

Although documents and diagrams in digital form can be passed around, an actual product or component cannot be passed around

Lack of face-to-face contact may mean a discussion may not be as effective

If the delegates are in distant locations, there can be a time lag, which can be distracting

Test yourself

Student book page 50

A wireless

B intranet

C network interface card

D bridge

E local

F wide

G router

H WLAN

I Wi-Fi

J bridge

K Bluetooth

L synchronise

M wireless

N spyware

O encryption

P antivirus

Q attachments

R download

S passwords

Exam-style questions

Student book page 51

1 One mark for each correct answer.

a Hub

b Intranet

c Extranet

d Network interface card

2 One mark for each correct answer.

A router – to enable data to be transferred from one network to another

A browser – to enable web pages to be viewed on the World Wide Web

Email – so that messages can be sent to people who are external to the home network

An ISP – in order to be able to access the internet/In order to be able to send emails to users outside the home network

3 a One mark for network interface card

b One mark for each of the following up to a maximum of two marks:

Reduced cabling costs

Reduced installation costs because there are fewer cables to lay

Very easy to connect extra devices to the network

Computers can connect to the network anywhere in the building provided there is a signal

c One mark for each of the following up to a maximum of two marks:

Can only be used to transfer data when the distances are small

The rate of data transfer is very slow compared to a wired network

Greater risk of the interception of data from hackers

Only supports a limited number of devices in a network

d One mark for the reason and one mark for a further detail × 3.

They may be worried that unauthorised users could get onto the network and compromise the security of the network by viewing/altering/deleting data.

Data such as bank account details could be stolen by hackers and used to commit fraud.

Spyware could be used to log keystrokes so that passwords could be obtained.

There could be accidental loss of data due to inexperienced operators, which could result in not being paid.

Without proper access controls, employees could access the payroll files and learn how much each employee earned.

A virus could be introduced onto the network which could result in the damage or deletion of important payroll files.

e One mark each for three of the following:

Use biometrics (e.g. retinal scanning, fingerprinting) for access control

Encrypt data

Use a system of usernames and passwords

Install antivirus software

Introduce a firewall

Use physical security such as locks on doors; security guards

Install antispyware

Use a proxy server

Don't allow the internal network to connect to the internet

4 One mark each for any five from the following:

LAN stands for local area network

WAN stands for wide area network

LAN is used in a limited geographical area, in one building or on one site

WAN is used over a wide geographical area spanning towns/countries

It is more difficult to share peripherals (e.g. scanners and printers) using a WAN

WANs consist of many LANs linked together

WANs usually use expensive telecommunications equipment which is hired from telecommunications companies

5 a One mark for:

A method used to transfer data over short distances wirelessly

b One mark each for three devices:

Speakers

Mouse

Keyboard

Smartphone

Headphones

Microphone

6 a One mark for each correctly placed tick:

It is possible to hold meetings at short notice.	√
It is cheaper as companies do not have to pay for travel expenses.	√
Fewer workers need to be employed.	

It is possible for employees to work from home.	√
You can hand around documents at a face-to-face meeting.	
You get to meet more people using video-conferencing.	

b One mark for each correctly placed tick.

Companies have to hire a large theatre to hold the meetings.	
Video-conferencing may not be as effective as face-to-face meetings.	√
Most people prefer personal contact rather than contact at a distance.	√
You cannot hand around documents or show presentations.	
Time differences in different countries can cause problems.	√
You can only show the presenter and not the delegates at the meeting.	

7 One mark for each correctly placed word:

	TRUE	FALSE
A data protection act helps prevent personal data from being misused by organisations.	True	
A memorable word should be chosen as a password as it is easy to remember.		False
Passwords should be changed regularly to deter hackers.	True	
Data protection principles are part of most data protection acts.	True	
Passwords should always be written down in case you forget them.		False

8 One mark for each point up to a maximum of five marks:

The screen is larger and easier to see with a desktop so it is more suited for working over a longer period of time.

With a desktop you are confined to a desk whereas with a smartphone you can work anywhere that has a signal.

Usually websites to be viewed on smartphones are not full versions.

It is easier to use the keyboard with a desktop rather than the onscreen one on a smartphone.

Access speeds are greater with a desktop as internet access wirelessly is generally slower than when using a cable.

You are reliant on the signal strength with a smartphone so there may be places where internet access is impossible.

9 **a** Switch – a device which inspects packages of data sent between computers so that it only sends packets to the computer they are intended for and not all the computers

b Router – device which decides which path a particular packet of data should take so that it arrives at its destination in the least possible time

10 One mark for each of five benefits/drawbacks:

Benefits:

It is possible to hold meeting at short notice.

It is cheaper as companies do not have to pay for travel expenses.

It is possible for employees to work from home.

Drawbacks:

Video-conferencing may not be as effective as face-to-face meetings.

Most people prefer personal contact rather than contact at a distance.

Time differences in different countries can cause problems.

11 One mark for each similarity (to a maximum of three) and one mark for each difference (to a maximum of three):

Similarities

Both are used to communicate/transfer data between devices.

Both are wireless technologies.

Both use radio frequencies.

Both have added security features.

Differences

Wi-Fi has a greater range (typically 100 m compared to 10 m).

Wi-Fi has a higher rate of data transmission.

Bluetooth is simpler to use and switching between devices is easier.

Wi-Fi can be used to connect a greater number of users.

Wi-Fi is more secure as it uses WEP (Wired Equivalency Privacy) and WPA (Wi-Fi Protected Access) together.

12 One mark each for five points:

The firewall controls incoming and outgoing data traffic

It prevents users on the network accessing undesirable sites

Stops unauthorised people using the internet to access networks

Stops users from downloading programs onto the network

Warns users trying to access sites with known security issues

Helps prevent malware being downloaded onto the network

Keeps a register of sites that users of the network are able to access

13 One mark each for six points:

Uses user_ID + password and another method to authenticate a user

Username and password + a physical object such as a credit/debit card/smartcard

Username and password + a one-time code sent to a user's phone by text message

Username and password + a token which can be a physical device such as a dongle inserted into the USB port of the user's computer or a radio frequency ID (RFID) chip

Username and password + a biometric method that make use of a user's physical characteristics such as fingerprint, iris/retina, voice recognition or face recognition

Worksheet 4.1: Networks wordsearch

Teacher resource pack page 32

1. Encryption
2. Hackers
3. Backup
4. Scrambles
5. Protection
6. Biometric
7. Internet
8. Intranet
9. Router
10. Radio

N	O	P	K	U	H	L	T	Z	S	E	J	S	W	S
N	O	P	U	H	L	E	Q	E	T	N	U	G	N	I
N	Z	I	U	K	N	N	L	L	D	C	W	Q	E	C
W	R	H	T	A	C	B	H	J	F	R	C	V	J	T
D	V	E	R	C	M	A	E	E	I	Y	I	X	M	H
T	T	T	T	A	E	Y	B	H	C	P	Y	Y	R	U
L	N	Q	R	U	R	T	B	R	G	T	G	L	B	P
I	A	C	Z	H	O	A	O	T	H	I	L	L	U	T
L	S	H	W	E	R	R	D	R	K	O	L	B	I	R
T	E	N	R	E	T	N	I	I	P	N	C	W	Z	C
H	E	K	O	O	N	F	E	Y	O	W	Y	S	M	C
C	F	H	X	B	B	O	U	L	D	B	O	M	E	S
P	W	R	H	A	C	K	E	R	S	J	D	U	S	H
C	I	R	T	E	M	O	I	B	U	D	D	C	L	A
A	U	I	Q	N	L	I	F	P	I	N	D	J	L	D

The effects of using IT

This worksheet can be best used following study of the effects of using IT in Chapter 5 of the Student Book.

Worksheet 5.1

Can you work out what the word is?

Here are some words or phrases which have been jumbled up. The words are connected with the effects of using IT. Can you work out what they are? There is a clue to help you.

1 decompress

Hint: Working longer hours over fewer days is called working ______ hours.

Answer: ____________________

2 time trap

Hint: Not working full time.

Answer: ____________________

3 back each

Hint: You may get this health problem if you do not sit up straight in your chair when using a computer.

Answer: ____________________

4 chase head

Hint: You might get these if you spend too long looking at the screen without a break.

Answer: ____________________

5 bet wise

Hint: There is an increase in employment for this type of designer.

Answer: ____________________

6 conductor pair

Hint: Someone who carries out this type of work in a factory may find their job is replaced by a robot.

Answer: ____________________

Worksheet 5.1 (continued)

7 job has grin

Hint: This involves sharing your job with others.

Answer: ______________________________

8 every lid

Hint: As more goods are sent to peoples' homes, employment for this type of driver has increased.

Answer: ______________________________

9 germs pram or

Hint: This type of job has increased due to the use of ICT.

Answer: ______________________________

10 sob rot

Hint: The use of these microprocessor-controlled devices in the home could make you lazy.

Answer: ______________________________

This activity can be best used following study of potential health problems related to use of ICT equipment in Chapter 5 on pages 54 to 55 of the Student Book.

Activity 5.1

Creating an interactive presentation on health and safety issues at work

Every new employee of an organisation gets an induction pack when they start work at the organisation. Part of this induction pack consists of some health and safety training on the safe use of ICT equipment.

You have been asked to produce a presentation using presentation software.

There are a number of requirements of the presentation and these are:

- The presentation is intended to be used by one employee at a time sitting at a computer.
- The presentation must be easy to use as they will be working on their own.
- It should be possible for the user to decide what they want to do next, so you will need some form of navigation around the presentation.
- The presentation should be fun to use.
- The target audience will be employees so your presentation must meet their needs.
- Appropriate images should be included.

You could try including some health and safety video if you can find a source.

Topic 5 answers

Questions A

Student book page 54

1 **a** One each for the names of three devices such as:

Central heating controller/Air conditioning controller

Microwave oven

Washing machine

Dishwasher

etc.

b One mark for each improvement up to a maximum of three marks such as:

Central heating controller/Air conditioning controller - can keep the room at a steady temperature all year

Microwave oven - food is cooked at the right level and for the correct time using details in the barcode

Washing machine - program washes the clothes, leaving you free to do other tasks or relax

Dishwasher - frees you from washing and drying dishes to do other things

2 One mark for each correct statement.

	TRUE	FALSE
Robots in the home can do all the housework.		False
Vacuuming robots can vacuum floors without anyone being present.	True	
Microprocessor-controlled devices in the home free up more leisure time for the occupants.	True	
The use of robots in the home will reduce the amount of exercise people get doing housework.	True	
People can become lazy if they rely on machines to perform all their tasks for them.	True	

3 One mark for each advantage/disadvantage up to a maximum of five marks:

Makes people less fit as exercise through cleaning, etc. is reduced

Makes people lazy if all their jobs can be performed by machines

Use of computers and smartphones may make people have less time for family life

People can use the time they save to do things they really want to do

It is easier to make new friends using social media sites than traditional methods of meeting

Questions B

Student book page 55

1 **a** One mark for each of three health problems (no mark for a one-word answer) such as:

Backache caused by incorrect posture when sitting in a chair

Repetitive strain injury (RSI) caused by typing at high speed

Eye strain caused by focusing on the screen for too long

b One mark for each of six points such as:

Use an adjustable chair (in work this may be a legal requirement but you need to ensure that the chair you use at home is adjustable).

Always check the adjustment of the chair to make sure it is suitable for your height - use a foot support (called a footrest) if necessary.

Sit up straight on the chair with your feet flat on the floor.

Make sure the screen is lined up and tilted at an appropriate angle.

Use appropriate lighting and blinds to avoid glare, which can cause headaches.

Take regular breaks to give your eyes a rest.

Have regular eye tests (if you use a screen in your work, then your employer may be required by law to pay for regular eye tests and glasses if they are needed).

Ensure you are not sitting too near the screen to avoid the possible risks of radiation.

2 **a** One mark for: repetitive strain injury

b One mark for one of the following:

Aches and pains in hands

Aches and pains in wrists

Aches and pains in arms

c One mark each for two of the following precautions:

Adjust the chair to the correct seating position for you.

Make sure there is enough space to work comfortably.

Use a document holder.

Use a wrist rest.

Keep wrists straight when keying in.

Position the mouse so that it can be used keeping the wrist straight.

Learn how to type properly - two-finger typing has been found to be much worse for RSI.

3 One mark for each correct answer:

a TRUE

b FALSE

c TRUE

d TRUE

e FALSE

Test yourself

Student book page 56

A car

B vacuuming

C health

D headaches

E back ache

F RSI

G blinds

H eye-tests

Exam-style questions

Student book page 57

1 **a** One mark for: repetitive strain injury

b One mark for each point up to a maximum of two marks:

Caused by typing for long periods or using a mouse over a long period of time

Caused by working in cramped conditions

Caused by repeatedly moving head a certain way to read a document and look at the screen

c One mark for one of the following:

Adjust your chair to the correct seating position for you.

Make sure there is enough space to work comfortably.

Use a document holder.

Use an ergonomic keyboard/mouse.

Use a wrist rest.

Keep your wrists straight when keying in.

Position the mouse so that it can be used keeping the wrist straight.

Learn how to type properly – two-finger typing has been found to be much worse for RSI.

2 One mark each for:

Backache

Repetitive strain injury (RSI)

Eye strain

3 **a** One mark for each of two health problems (not eye strain or RSI) such as:

Backache

Neck ache

Headaches

b One mark each for two methods of prevention:

Backache – use an adjustable chair and make sure you adjust it to suit your height – you can use a foot rest if there is one.

Neck ache – ensure the screen is positioned in front of the user/ensure a copyholder is used.

Headache – make sure that fluorescent tubes are used with diffusers on them to spread out the light.

4 **a** One mark for the health hazard and one mark for the health problem × 3.

RSI – a painful condition of the hands and wrists

Backache and neck ache – painful condition when moving

Eye strain – blurred vision

Headaches – pain in head and blurred vision

b One mark each for three methods such as:

RSI – take frequent breaks

Backache and neck ache – adopt the correct posture (i.e. sit up straight)

Eye strain – have frequent eye tests and wear glasses/contact lenses if needed

Headaches – ensure screen is clear and make sure there is no glare on the screen

5 One mark for each of four points:

Ability to share jobs – more flexibility is needed as businesses operate longer hours, so this has become popular with employers.

Ability to work compressed hours – many people prefer to work longer hours over fewer days because it cuts down travel costs, etc.

Greater availability of part-time work – many employers need staff 24 hours a day and this increases the opportunity for part-time work.

Flexible hours – staff are needed who are not restricted to working normal office hours.

6 One mark each from two possible health problems such as:

Eye strain

Headaches

Backache

One mark each for two correct precautions such as:

Eye strain – have frequent eye tests and wear glasses/contact lenses if needed.

Headaches – ensure screen is clear and make sure there is no glare on the screen.

Backache – adopt the correct posture (i.e. sit up straight).

7 One mark for each of five effects such as:

You do not need be around when the vacuuming or floor washing takes place.

You do not need to be in the house when washing is being washed.

Microprocessor-controlled alarm systems can help you feel safe.

You have more time to spend with your family.

Microprocessor-controlled fitness machines can help you keep fit without leaving home to go to the gym.

Machines doing manual tasks can result in people not getting enough exercise.

Ease at which ready meals can be cooked can lead to unhealthy eating habits.

Worksheet 5.1: Can you work out what the word is?

Teacher resource pack page 41

1. Compressed
2. Part time
3. Backache
4. Headaches
5. Website
6. Car production
7. Job sharing
8. Delivery
9. Programmers
10. Robots

6 ICT applications

This worksheet can be best used following study of ICT applications in Chapter 6 of the Student Book.

Worksheet 6.1

Applications crossword

Complete the crossword using the clues on the next page.

Worksheet 6.1 (continued)

Across

2. Method used to record the attendance of a student automatically using a property of the human body such as fingerprints
3. Continually taking measurements and comparing them with a pre-set value
4. Name given to the process banks used for sorting out cheque payments
7. Medical expert systems are used for this
8. Values from a sensor that are continually varying
9. Using mathematical equations to mimic a real situation such as family finances

Down

1. The 'P' in VOIP
3. The characters on a bank cheque are printed in this type of ink
5. The part of an expert system a user interacts with
6. Type of system used to switch a heater off when it gets too hot and on when it gets too cold

This activity can be best used following study of modelling on pages 62 and 63 of Chapter 6, and of spreadsheets in Chapter 20, in the Student Book.

Activity 6.1

Producing a spreadsheet model to simulate depreciation

When you drive a new car out of the showroom it will go down in price. If you tried to sell it back to a garage or privately, you will get less than you paid for it. As you use the car and it gets older, its value goes down. This is called depreciation.

Cars depreciate at different rates depending on the make and model. BMWs and Mercedes depreciate less than Fords or Vauxhalls, although they generally cost more to buy in the first place.

In this activity we will try to produce a model for the depreciation for two different new cars over a four-year period:

Car A has a depreciation of 40% per year whilst car B has a depreciation of only 25% per year.

The costs of each car when new are: Car A $13000   Car B $18500

Follow these steps to set up the model.

1 Load the spreadsheet software until you see the blank grid. Now type in the data exactly in the positions shown here:

	A	B	C	D	E	F	G	H
1	A model showing car depreciation							
2				Year 1	Year 2	Year 3	Year 4	
3	Car A	$13,000						
4	Car B	$18,500						
5								
6								

2 In cell D3 type in the formula = 0.6*b3

This will calculate 60% of the original price (i.e. 100% - 40% = 60% depreciation which can be written 60/100 or 0.6).

Check that it now looks like this:

	A	B	C	D	E	F	G	H
1	A model showing car depreciation							
2				Year 1	Year 2	Year 3	Year 4	
3	Car A	$13,000		$7,800.0				
4	Car B	$18,500						
5								
6								

3 In cell E3 type in the formula =0.6*d3

This works out 60% of the price after year 1.

In cell F3 type in the formula =0.6*e3

In cell G3 type in the formula = 0.6*f3

Activity 6.1 (continued)

Check that the spreadsheet now looks like this:

	A	B	C	D	E	F	G	H
1	A model showing car depreciation							
2				Year 1	Year 2	Year 3	Year 4	
3	Car A	$13,000		$7,800.0	$4,680.0	$2,808.0	$1,684.80	
4	Car B	$18,500						
5								

4 For Car B, the depreciation is 25%. This means that the car is worth 100% - 25% = 75% of its price the previous year.

You have to construct the formulae in a similar way to step 3 using the figure 0.75 to fill in the amounts for Year 1, Year 2, etc.

Your spreadsheet will now look like this:

	A	B	C	D	E	F	G	H
1	A model showing car depreciation							
2				Year 1	Year 2	Year 3	Year 4	
3	Car A	$13,000		$7,800.0	$4,680.0	$2,808.0	$1,684.80	
4	Car B	$18,500		$13,875.00	$10,406.25	$7,804.69	$5,853.52	
5								

5 We can now work out how much the cars have depreciated in total over the four years. In cell H2 put the heading 'Depreciation' (you will need to widen the column to fit in the text).

To work out the total depreciation for Car A we subtract the figure in cell G3 from the figure in cell B3. Put the formula =B3-G3 in cell H3.

Put a similar formula =B4-G4 in cell H4.

The final model will look like this:

	A	B	C	D	E	F	G	H
1	A model showing car depreciation							
2				Year 1	Year 2	Year 3	Year 4	Depreciation
3	Car A	$13,000		$7,800.0	$4,680.0	$2,808.0	$1,684.80	$11,315.20
4	Car B	$18,500		$13,875.00	$10,406.25	$7,804.69	$5,853.52	$12,646.48
5								

6 We can now alter the prices and see what happens to the depreciation. Suppose both cars cost exactly the same price but still had the same rates of depreciation. What would happen if they both cost $15000? Put the value $15000 into cells B3 and B4.

The model now looks like this:

	A	B	C	D	E	F	G	H
1	A model showing car depreciation							
2				Year 1	Year 2	Year 3	Year 4	Depreciation
3	Car A	$15,000		$9000.0	$5,400.0	$3,2408.0	$1,9440.00	$13,056.00
4	Car B	$15,000		$11,250.00	$8,437.50	$6,328.13	$4,746.09	$10,253.91
5								

This activity can be best used following study of modelling on pages 62 and 63 of Chapter 6, and of spreadsheets in Chapter 20, in the Student Book.

Activity 6.2

Making the model more useful

This car depreciation model is fairly simple. We can alter the prices of the cars fairly easily but it is quite difficult to change the depreciation rate because it is part of each formula. What we need are two cells where you input the depreciation rate for each car.

Different cars have different depreciation rates. It would be an idea to work out the accurate depreciation rates for different cars using accurate data. You can get data about prices for cars from websites such as Parkers.

You may also like to look into whether the depreciation rate changes from one year to the next. If this could be built into the model it would reflect the real situation and make the model more accurate.

This worksheet can be best used following study of the applications of ICT on pages 63 to 77 of Chapter 6 in the Student Book.

Worksheet 6.2

Computers in control?

There are many places where you can find computers in control. Computers can switch things on and off automatically. They can work through a process without the need for a human to be present.

Write your answers directly onto the worksheet.

Example 1 has been completed for you.

Place where you might find computers in control	Example 1	Example 2	Example 3
In your school	Central heating system		
In your home	Washing machine		
At a fairground/theme park	To count people passing through the turnstiles		
Along a road	Fog warning system		
In a shopping centre	Controlling the barrier in the car park		

This worksheet can be best used following study of the applications of ICT on pages 63 to 77 of Chapter 6 in the Student Book.

Worksheet 6.3

Describing how control is used

There are many places where control is used. For this worksheet you have to explain how control is used for each of the examples described.

To make it clear what you have to do, the first example has been done for you.

Place where you might find computers in control	Example	How control is used
In your school	Central heating system	To turn the heating on when the temperature, as measured by a sensor, falls below a set value. If the temperature rises above a different set value and the heating is on, then it will be turned off. This way the temperature remains fairly constant.
In your home	Washing machine	
At a fairground/theme park	To count people passing through the turnstiles	
Along a road	Fog warning system	
In a shopping centre	Controlling the barrier in the car park	

This activity can be best used following study of applications in manufacturing industries on page 63 of Chapter 6 in the Student Book.

Activity 6.3

Researching the use of robots

For this activity you have to use the internet for research to find out about as many different uses for robots as you can.

You then have to produce a document which contains a picture of the robot along with a brief explanation as to how it is used.

To help you understand what you have to do, the first one has been done for you.

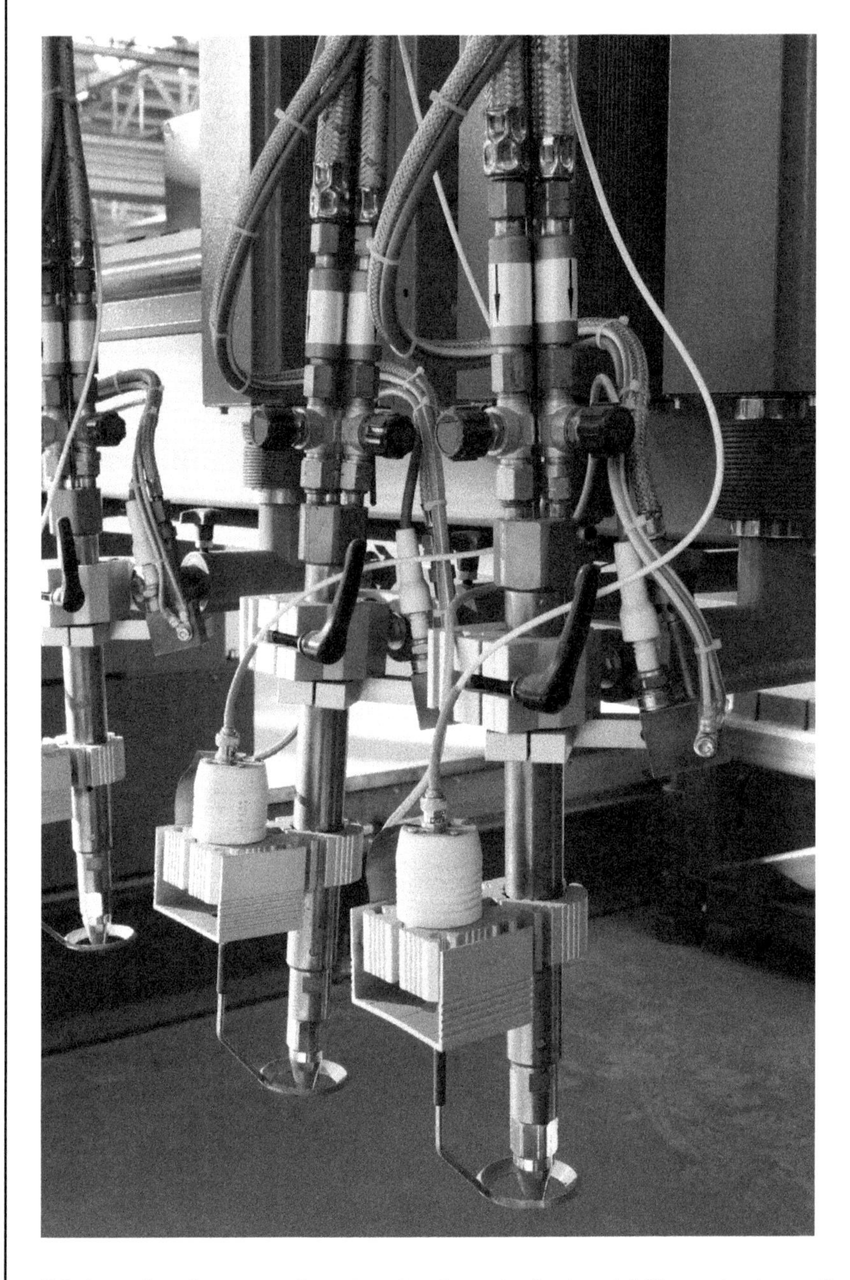

This is a robot that uses a laser to cut patterns in sheet metal. These sheets are then shaped to form the panels for car bodies. The panels are then welded together, also by a robot.

Topic 6 answers

Questions A

Student book page 59

1 a One mark for: Voice over Internet Protocol

b Two marks for:

Cheap international telephone calls can be made

2 One mark for each method up to a maximum of three marks

Email

VoIP

SMS/Text messaging

Voicemail

Electronic faxing

Social networking sites

Instant messaging

etc.

Questions B

Student book page 62

1 Marks according to the following:

No mistakes in instructions = 4 marks

1 mistake = 3 marks

2–3 mistakes = 2 marks

4–5 mistakes = 1 mark

>5 mistakes = 0 marks

FORWARD 50

RIGHT 90

FORWARD 25

PENUP

FORWARD 50

PENDOWN

FORWARD 25

RIGHT 90

FORWARD 50

RIGHT 90

FORWARD 100

2 a One mark for the name and one mark for a description of what it does × 2.

Moisture – so that the amount of water in the soil can be determined in case it is too dry.

Humidity – the moisture in the air can be measured so that a fine mist can be turned on or off.

Light – the light is measured and controls the blinds.

pH – to control the acidity/alkalinity of the soil.

b One mark for each advantage up to a maximum of two marks:

The system is completely automatic

No wage costs for people to water plants

c One mark for one disadvantage such as:

High initial cost of buying the equipment

Equipment needs to be maintained

Equipment can malfunction which can cause plant loss

Causes unemployment among staff who used to look after plants manually

3 One mark for each of three output devices such as:

Motor

Actuator

Heater

Lamp/Light

4 a Two sensors (one mark each) such as:

Pressure

Temperature

Humidity

Rainfall

Light/Sun – to record hours of sunlight

b One mark for a method and one mark for further amplification:

The data is sent wirelessly through the air and it is picked up by a receiver inside or attached to the computer.

c One mark for a method and an extra mark for further detail:

It is displayed on a small LCD screen in the form of icons (such as sun/rain, etc.).

It is displayed graphically.

Graphs are drawn to show the way the quantity measured has changed.

Questions C

Student book page 66

1 a Two marks for:

As the user enters the booking details the seat is saved for them so as to prevent double booking.

b One mark each for two of the following:

Booking seats online is usually cheaper as the airline does not have to pay a commission.

You can book the tickets from anywhere and at any time.

There is no need to collect tickets as they can be printed on your own printer.

You have more time to make decisions about flights.

c One mark each for two of the following:

Need to use a credit/debit card online and the details may not be kept safe

People could hack into the site and find out when you were away from home

You could easily make a mistake and book the wrong flight

There is no person to ask if you get stuck

2 a One mark for each of two features:

Being able to produce timetables

Being able to organise examinations

Being able to store student details

Being able to store and produce statistics on attendance

b One mark for an advantage such as:

They reduce the workload for teachers.

They support decision making for school managers.

They can help reduce truancy.

c One mark for a disadvantage such as:

They are expensive to purchase.

Software is complex so a lot of training is needed to use it.

They must ensure that there is no unauthorised access as a lot of personal data is stored.

3 Two marks for an advantage and further explanation × 2.

Biometric methods mean that the form teacher does not have to register each student. This allows them more time to talk with the students.

Other people can access the registration details at the same time if needed. For example, a head teacher might meet with a parent to discuss absences whilst the form teacher was registering students.

4 a One mark for each of two tasks such as:

Paint spraying the panels of cars on the production line of a car factory

Welding car panels together to create the body of a car in a car factory

Assembling components such as the parts of an engine in a car factory

b One mark for each of three advantages such as:

More accurate than a human

Do not need to be paid wages so cheaper

Robots can work continuously without a break

Robots can work in poor environments where it would not be healthy to allow a human to work

c One mark for each of three disadvantages such as:

Causes unemployment as some jobs are replaced

Robots have a high initial cost

Robots need to be programmed precisely to work properly

Questions D

Student book page 68

1 a One mark each for:

Credit card

Debit card

b One mark for each point made to a maximum of four marks.

Chip and PIN was introduced because all you had to do previously was sign a form. The signature was compared with a stored signature to verify that you were the true owner of the card. Signatures were easily forged. Now a number called a PIN is encrypted in the chip on the card and the reader asks the user to enter the PIN. Only the true owner of the card knows the PIN so this cuts down the fraudulent use of stolen cards.

2 a One mark for each of two ways such as:

Can be used as evidence of identity to take out loans/credit cards

Can be used to purchase goods and services

Can be used to obtain cash from ATMs if the PIN is known

b One mark for an answer similar to the following:

Use of chip and PIN where the user has to enter a series of numbers which only they should know

3 a One mark for electronic funds transfer

b One mark each for two advantages and one mark each for two disadvantages.

Advantages:

You can transfer money between accounts on any device with internet access.

The transfer of money is fast.

The transfer is secure as it is subject to a high degree of data encryption.

Funds can be sent to anyone who has a bank account anywhere in the world.

Disadvantages:

There is a danger that hackers could intercept the transfer.

The charges for the service can be high.

A mistake in the entry of one of the very long account numbers could result in the money being transferred to the wrong account.

4 One mark each for three services such as:

Hear the balance of your account

Check your latest transactions (i.e. what money has gone into and come out of your account)

Pay a credit card bill

Transfer money between different accounts you hold at the same bank

Listen to details of standing orders and direct debits

Questions E

Student book page 69

1 a One mark for each of three sensors:

Temperature, blood pressure, pulse, central venous pressure, blood sugar and brain activity

b One mark for each of two uses:

Expert systems for diagnosis

Computerised reporting of laboratory tests

Pharmacy records

Organising patient appointments

Keeping patient records

2 a One mark for each of three quantities:

Temperature, blood pressure, pulse, central venous pressure, blood sugar and brain activity

b i One mark for analogue to digital converter

ii To convert the continually variable analogue signals from the sensor and convert them into digital signals that can be processed by the computer

3 One mark for each correctly placed tick.

	√
Nurses cannot take readings accurately.	
Nurses cannot take readings at the correct time.	
Sensors attached to computers can take readings more regularly.	√
Computer monitoring can take place all the time and not at certain intervals.	√
Printouts from the computer make it easier to spot trends in the patient's condition.	√
Computers can measure more than one physical quantity at the same time.	√
It is cheaper to use a computer system rather than employ lots of nurses.	√
Continual monitoring is safer than monitoring only now and again	√

4 a One mark for analogue to digital converter

b Points similar to the following to a maximum of five marks.

The sensor measures the temperature which is sent to the processor which then compares the reading with the pre-set value. The pre-set value is the temperature setting the user makes. If the read temperature is less than the pre-set value, the heater is turned on and if it is less, the heater is turned off.

Questions F

Student book page 71

1 One mark for each correct answer.

	TRUE	FALSE
RFID uses radio signals to communicate with the reader.	True	
The reader and the RFID must be in contact for the reader to read the data off the chip.		False
RFID is used in library management systems.	True	
RFID does not make use of an aerial.		False
RFID is replacing barcodes in library management systems.	True	
Using RFID, books can be returned when the library is closed.	True	
RFID makes use of magnetic ink characters.		False

2 a One mark for each point to a maximum of four marks:

The RFID chip in the books identifies the book to the system which can be used to link with a borrower using their card. The RFID chip can be read at a distance which means people can return books through a drop-off box when the library is closed.

b One mark for each of two points such as:

RFID works at a distance which means that books can be dropped off when the library is closed

RFID holds a lot more information compared to a barcode

Can be used in conjunction with a security system which stops books being removed without being properly checked out

Questions G

Student book page 72

1 a Any two (one mark each) from the following:

Knowledge base

Rules base

Inference engine

User interface

b One mark for one of the following:

More accurate diagnosis

Fewer mistakes as computers do not forget things

Cheaper than employing a consultant or expert

c One mark for one of the following:

Can check what they think with what the expert system thinks/get second opinion

Patient may answer questions more truthfully if they are asked the questions by a computer

d One mark for one of the following:

Lacks common sense

Lacks senses (e.g. can't tell pain from patient's body language)

Only as good as the person who set it up

They are very expensive to create

2 a One mark for each of two points similar to the following:

ICT systems that are designed to replace a human expert in a particular field

It uses artificial intelligence to make decisions

Decisions are based on applying a series of rules to a body of knowledge

b One mark each for two points similar to the following:

They can use the system to help them make a correct diagnosis.

They can use the system to confirm a diagnosis.

They can use the system when they feel they do not know enough about the illness.

3 a One mark for each of two jobs similar to the following:

Doctors

Architects

Geologists

Accountants

b One mark each for two descriptions for each job referred to in part (a):

Doctors for medical diagnosis

Architects for the designing of buildings

Geologists for prospecting for minerals and oil

Accountants for giving tax advice to individuals and companies

4 One mark for the use and one mark for further explanation such as:

A financial advisor for a bank who advises on the best mortgage based on their client's circumstances

5 a One mark for one of the following:

More accurate diagnosis of the particular blood infection

Fewer mistakes as computers do not forget things such as the symptoms of various blood infections

Cheaper than employing a consultant or expert in blood disorders

b One mark for one of the following:

Lacks common sense so it can only come to a diagnosis based on the answers to the questions

Lacks senses (e.g. can't tell pain from patient's body language) so the system would not be able to tell anything from the appearance of the patient or the way they reacted

Only as good as the person who set it up so the person setting the system up would need a high level of medical as well as IT skills

Questions H

Student book page 74

1 a One method for one mark such as:

Credit card

Debit card

PayPal

b Two marks for answers such as:

They are worried about identity theft.

They are worried that their card details could be found and used fraudulently.

c Two marks for answers such as:

Credit/debit card details are encrypted

Which means they are scrambled when sent or stored

Which prevents others understanding them

2 a One mark each for two advantages such as:

The goods are usually cheaper.

It is much easier to shop around so you get the best price.

You can use comparison sites to get the best price.

You can see what others say about the service offered by the online store.

The goods are delivered straight to your door.

You can buy goods from anywhere in the world.

You do not waste time looking for goods that might be out of stock.

b One mark each for two disadvantages such as:

If you want the goods urgently you may still have to wait for delivery.

It is sometimes necessary to see and touch what you are buying.

It is a hassle to send goods back.

Sometimes the customer service is not as good as a traditional store.

There are fake stores where you pay for goods that never arrive.

People may be worried about using their credit/debit card details to pay for goods owing to identity theft.

c i One mark each for two suitable stores such as:

Supermarkets

Clothes stores

Bookshops

CD/DVD stores

ii One mark each for two similar to:

High street bookshops

High street record stores

Corner shops

High street travel agents

3 One mark for each detailed point (not just a name) to a maximum of six.

Goods or services are usually cheaper on the internet.

Organisations find it cheaper to use the internet, as they do not need as many staff, they do not need expensive premises and some of these savings can be passed to the customer.

Online catalogues can be viewed. Products can be searched for by a large number of criteria.

There is a much bigger choice of products. Internet bookshops have huge stocks of books compared to a local bookshop.

Product reviews can be obtained before you buy. For example, you can see what other people who have bought a book say about it before you buy.

Orders can be placed on the internet 24 hours a day, 7 days a week, 52 weeks per year.

You can buy software/music over the internet and receive it by downloading it. This can be less effort than having to order it by mail order or by travelling to a shop to buy it.

You can use price comparison sites to ensure that the goods are bought for the best price.

Once the customer has made an initial order, the customer details such as name, address, credit card details can be stored and therefore do not need to be entered again. This makes shopping online very fast.

Supermarkets who deliver to the home also keep a shopping list of items that you order regularly so you just need to make changes in this list.

You can buy goods anywhere in the world.

Questions I

Student book page 75

1 a One mark for an answer such as:

They can ensure they are just doing work-related tasks

To ensure that they are not doing things (e.g. downloading games) that could expose the organisation to a virus attack

To ensure they are not doing something illegal (e.g. breaching copyright)

b One mark for an answer such as:

To ensure they are dealing properly with customers, etc.

To ensure they are not sending emails not related to work

2 a One mark for each of three points such as:

The camera takes the picture and then uses OCR software to recognise and record the registration plate details which can be used, for example, for raising a car park barrier to only allow authorised cars in or to send fines to speeding cars.

b One mark for:

Removes them from routine tasks such as parking, speeding, jumping red lights, etc., thus enabling them to concentrate on other work

c One mark each for two uses such as:

Spotting cars on the road without tax/insurance

Issuing speeding fines automatically

Issuing parking fines automatically

3 a One mark for camera

b Three marks for answers similar to the following:

Camera takes a picture of the number plate, OCR software is used to recognise the number as individual characters which are then looked for in a database of cars that are allowed entry.

c One mark for one advantage such as:

No staff wages need to be paid.

There is no ticket/card for the driver to forget.

The barrier can operate 24 hours per day without a break.

Questions J

Student book page 77

1 One mark for each correct answer.

	TRUE	FALSE
GPS stands for global positioning service.		False
GPS uses a single satellite.		False
GPS is only accurate to 10 m.		False
GPS cannot be used for the navigation of aircraft.		False
GPS cannot be used for walkers as it does not work in remote places.		False
GPS is used by surveyors for accurately marking out plots of land.	True	
It is only possible to use GPS in satellite navigation systems.		False

2 a One mark for: global positioning system

b One mark for a map

c One mark for either touch screen or microphone (for voice recognition)

d One mark each for three of the following:

Finding the distance between two places

Producing an aerial view of an area

Marking out a plot of land accurately

3 a One mark each for three points such as:

Accurate instructions are given so you don't get lost, which saves on time and fuel and reduces the stress of having to read a map.

b One mark each for three points such as:

The system may be out of date and not show roads that have been built recently.

It make take you along a road that is unsuitable for your vehicle.

Programming your route into the system whilst driving is dangerous.

4 a Any three marks allocated in a similar way to:

GPS stands for global positioning system. GPS is a satellite-based system which uses at least four satellites to work out the distance between the receiver and each of the satellites, in order to work out the position (i.e. latitude, longitude and altitude) of the receiver on the Earth.

b One mark for each of two ways:

Used in conjunction with a map to produce a satellite navigation system

Finding the distance between two places

Producing an aerial view of an area

Marking out a plot of land accurately

Test yourself

Student book page 78

A internet

B VoIP

C smartphones, emails

D expert

E knowledge base

F rules base

G user interface

H experts

I question

J diagnosis

K cheaper

L phone, internet

M ATM

N sensors, digital, analogue to digital converter

O pre-set

Revision questions

Student book page 78

1 a One mark for the name of a suitable device such as:

Washing machine

Dishwasher

Iron

Toaster

Alarm

b One mark for each of three points. Example answer for a washing machine control system might be:

Controls the flow of water into the machine

Heats the water up to the correct temperature

Uses the program to obey the set of instructions for a particular wash

Controls the pumps which pump the dirty water out of the machine

Controls when the detergent is added

Controls the spin speed

Controls how long the dryer cycle is on for

Releases the door hatch when it is safe to do so

2 a One mark each for three advantages such as:

The details are recorded instantly – teachers and admin staff can chase up non-attendees

Teachers have the admin burden removed – they can concentrate on teaching

Harder for students to abuse the system

Promotes health and safety – need to know who is in the school in case of an emergency

Can check attendance at each lesson

No need to physically move the registers

Takes up less space than paper-based registers

Attendance can be accessed from any computer connected to the school network

b One mark for each of three disadvantages such as:

The cost – biometric methods are quite expensive

Dependence on equipment which can sometimes fail

Privacy issues if fingerprinting is used

3 One mark for each of two points similar to the following:

Welding panels or components together

Assembling components

Spraying panels/cars, etc.

Packaging goods

Deep sea repairs to oil rigs

Mowing lawns

Vacuuming carpets/floors

etc.

4 a One mark for each service up to a maximum of three marks:

View bank statements

Transfer money between accounts

Make payments for bills

Apply for loans

b One mark for each up to a maximum of two marks:

Worry about inputting the wrong data

Worry about hackers accessing their banking details

Worry about others using their account fraudulently

c One mark for one of the following:

Worry about inputting the wrong data – bank can explain that range checks are used to check that huge amounts are not moved between accounts by mistake

Worry about hackers accessing their banking details – explain that banking details are encrypted when passing between banks and customers

Worry about others using their account fraudulently – explain how firewalls are used to keep personal details secure

5 One mark for each of five points which must be relevant to an internet booking system:

Using online processing

Online processing means that the booking is held while you

enter your personal and payment details and this prevents double booking

You get the confirmation immediately usually as an email which you can print out

Tickets/bookings are usually cheaper because there is no agent commission to pay

Can read reviews on the internet before booking

Can use comparison sites to determine where to buy the cheapest ticket

The tickets are sent by post to you or you can print them out, which saves time compared to picking them up

Can book without leaving your home

You can spend as much time as you like searching for flights, hotels, etc.

Exam-style questions

Student book page 79

1 One mark for each correct statement shown here:

PEN DOWN

LEFT 90

REPEAT 6

FORWARD 15

RIGHT 60

LEFT

END REPEAT

2 One mark each for four of the following:

The user interface asks questions on the screen.

The questions relate to the geology of the area.

The user answers these questions by keying in answers.

More questions are asked on the basis of previous answers.

The system suggests likely places where oil could be found.

Percentage probabilities of finding oil in these places are shown.

Suggested information regarding the depth of the deposits is shown.

Maps showing areas where oil might be found are displayed.

3 **a** One mark for each point to a maximum of six marks:

Interactive screen asks user to enter details.

Details such as make, model, engine size, etc. are entered.

Questions are then asked about the problem.

Answers are input at the keyboard.

The inference engine decides on the next question based on previous questions.

The knowledge base is searched using the rules base.

Problems are output on the screen.

The probabilities of each likely problem are displayed.

b One mark each for two of the following:

Mineral/oil prospecting

Medical diagnosis

Chess games

For giving tax advice to individuals and companies

For giving an insurance quote

For careers advice/guidance

4 **a** One mark for each of three sensors such as:

Temperature

Humidity

Moisture

Light

b **i** Two marks for a similar explanation:

Analogue data is constantly changing whereas digital data changes from one value to another without any in-between value.

ii Two marks for – computers are only able to process digital data.

c One mark each for three reasons such as:

Can work continuously 24 hours a day, 7 days a week

Readings can be taken more frequently so the conditions can be kept more constant

It is cheaper as no wages need to be paid

5 **a** One mark each for three sensors and one mark for their purpose such as:

Pressure – to fill the water to the correct depth

Force/Weight – to ensure that the drum has not been overloaded with washing

Temperature – to ensure the washing is washed at the correct temperature for the program chosen

Moisture – to ensure that the washing is dry when tumbled dried

b Five marks for five points explaining the use of the sensors:

Data from the weight/force sensor is sent to the processor which checks that the machine has not been overloaded with washing. If it has, it switches on a warning light. The water is allowed in and once the sensor measures that the water pressure has reached a pre-set value, the processor sends a signal to turn the water off. The heater then heats the water to the value programmed. The washing machine motor then obeys the instructions according to the program. The water is pumped out and the drying process starts and stops when the humidity sensor detects that the washing is dry.

6 One mark for each of two methods of input such as:

Barcodes

RFID chips/tags

RFID:

Three marks for advantages and disadvantages such as the following:

The tag and reader do not need to come into contact with each other so books can be returned when the library is closed.

More information about the book/lender can be stored on an RFID tag.

As the data can be read at a distance there is the danger that the system can be hacked into.

Barcode:

Barcodes are easily damaged

7 a One mark for each of three physical quantities:

Temperature, blood pressure, pulse, central venous pressure, blood sugar and brain activity

b One mark for each of three advantages such as:

Readings can be taken more frequently

Nurses could forget to take the readings but sensors will not forget

There is no human error when taking readings

The results can be obtained immediately by the computer plotting a graph to enable trends to be spotted

Frees up nurses to do non-routine tasks

Fewer nurses are needed so the wage bill will be less

Alarms can be sounded immediately if readings fall outside a certain range

8 One mark each for each of four differences such as:

With phone banking no access to the internet is needed.

With phone banking you can choose to speak to a human.

With phone banking you can get advice on banking services.

Access to banking services is almost instant with internet banking, but with phone banking you may have to wait in a queue to speak to an assistant.

9 a Three marks for an answer similar to the following:

The sensor measures temperatures which are analogue readings. The computer can only work with digital data so the analogue data needs to be converted into digital data using an analogue to digital converter which is the extra device needed.

b Points similar to the following to a maximum of four marks:

The sensor measures the temperature which is sent to the processor which then compares the reading with the pre-set value. The pre-set value is the temperature setting the user makes. If the read temperature is less than the pre-set value, the heater is turned on and if it is more, the heater is turned off, thus keeping the temperature of the room constant.

10 a One mark each for three variables such as:

Temperature

Pressure

Humidity

Hours of sunlight

Rainfall

b i Two marks

The signals from the sensors are analogue signals and as these are sent to the computer for processing they need to be converted into digital signals that the computer can understand.

ii One mark for analogue to digital converter

c One mark for each of three reasons such as:

No human error when taking readings

No missed readings due to the person who normally takes the readings being sick or on holiday

Readings can be input straight into the computer without the need for typing

More regular readings can be obtained because no-one needs to be present to take them

11 One mark for each of up to three advantages and three disadvantages:

Advantages

It is better for the environment – reduces the number of car/train/bus journeys.

It saves time – you do not waste time travelling, in queues.

You can bank 24/7.

It is easier to bank when you are away from home.

Internet-only banks often offer better interest rates as there are no high street premises to pay for.

You are physically safer as someone could follow you if you take cash to the bank or take it out.

It enables you to check your balance more regularly which means you can budget your money better.

One mark for each of ? disadvantages:

Disadvantages

You need a reliable internet connection.

There are security issues, particularly if you use an unsecured or Wi-Fi connection.

There is a greater risk of pharming, phishing, or other types of fraud.

A device such as a dongle is needed for two-factor authentication.

It is easy to make errors in account numbers, IBAN, sort codes, etc., which could result in money being transferred to the wrong account.

You can obtain or deposit cash/physical money using internet banking.

If you lose your internet connection during a transaction it can cause problems because you are unsure whether the transaction was completed.

12 One mark each for:

a B11

b =B3*E3 or + E3*B3

c =SUM(B6:B8) or =B6+B7+B8

d One mark for each of three reasons:

You can perform 'what if?' scenarios to see what happens.

Changing a single value results in all dependent values being automatically recalculated.

When you change a value you can see immediately how it changes other values.

13 One mark for each point to a maximum of three marks.

Teachers enter marks for homework, classwork, tests and details of skills learnt directly into the computer.

Results can be analysed using software which can compare the performance of the student against other students in the same class/year or students nationally.

Good and bad behaviour can be recorded.

Data is held centrally so all teachers can access it, which means a full picture of a student's progress can be obtained across all subjects.

Students and parents can see a student's progress or otherwise and take appropriate action.

14 One mark for each correctly placed tick.

	True	False
Cheque clearing uses magnetic characters which are read automatically using optical mark recognition.		✓
Cheques are sent to a clearing centre where they are processed.	✓	
It takes over two weeks to clear a cheque.		✓

15 a One mark for each correct answer:

magnetic ink character recognition and optical character recognition

b One mark for each of 3 advantages and one mark for each of 3 disadvantages:

Advantages of OCR:

Uses a smartphone as a reader which most people have

The readers are cheap compared to MICR readers

No need to physically present the cheque at the bank for reading

No delay in reading the cheque and transferring the information to the bank

A smartphone is a cheaper input device compared to a magnetic ink character reader

Cheaper to print characters in ordinary ink on cheques rather than in magnetic ink

Disadvantages of OCR:

MICR characters on a cheque are in magnetic ink so are difficult to forge whereas OCR characters are easier to forge

OCR characters are difficult to read if the cheque has been folded or torn

OCR reading speed is slower than MICR

Less secure than MICR

Easy to photocopy characters on the cheque and try to use them again fraudulently.

Worksheet 6.1: Applications crossword

Teacher resource pack page 47

1 Protocol **2** Biometric **3A** Monitoring
3D Magnetic **4** Clearing **5** Interface
6 Control **7** Diagnosis **8** Analogue
9 Modelling

Worksheet 6.2: Computers in control?

Teacher resource pack page 52

Place where you might find computers in control	Example 1	Example 2	Example 3
In your school	Central heating system	Burglar alarm system	Automatic watering system for the school playing fields
In your home	Washing machine	DVD recorder	Central heating system
At a fairground/theme park	To count people passing through the turnstiles	Metal detection system for security	To control the operation of a camera on a ride
Along a road	Fog warning system	Traffic light control system	Barrier system to control the entry to a car park
In a shopping centre	Controlling the barrier in the car park	Controlling the sprinkler system in case of fire	Controlling the heating/air conditioning

Worksheet 6.3: Describing how control is used

Teacher resource pack page 54

Place where you might find computers in control	Example	How control is used
In your school	Central heating system	To turn the heating on when the temperature, as measured by a sensor falls below a set value. If the temperature rises above a different set value and the heating is on, then it will be turned off. This way the temperature remains fairly constant.
In your home	Washing machine	To allow the right amount of water to enter. To heat the water up to a certain temperature, add the powder and wash for a certain time. To drain water and add more to rinse and then to empty the water and heat washing till it is dry.
At a fairground/ theme park	To count people passing through the turnstiles	To activate a counter each time the turnstile moves enough to allow a person to enter.
Along a road	Fog warning system	Light sensors will come on when there is fog obstructing the area between the light source and the light cell. When the sensor detects fog, the warning signs light up. When the fog clears, the warning signs are turned off automatically.
In a shopping centre	Controlling the barrier in the car park	When car approaches, a ticket is printed and on its removal, the barrier rises. The car is detected having passed the barrier and the barrier is instructed to close.

The systems life cycle

This worksheet can be best used following study of validation checks on page 84 of Chapter 7, and Chapter 20 Spreadsheets, in the Student Book.

Worksheet 7.1

Spreadsheet cell validation checks

Here are some validation checks which are to be applied to a range of cells in a worksheet created using spreadsheet software.

For each of the checks, give the name of the validation check and also give a brief explanation of how the check will help prevent incorrect data being entered.

1 Validation check 1

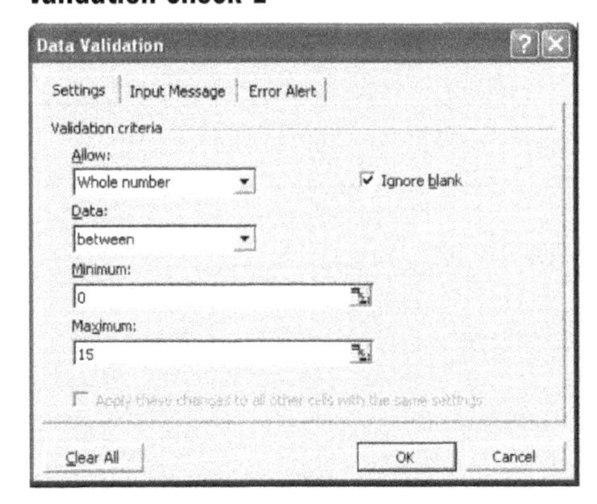

Name of validation check ______________________________

Explanation ______________________________

____

2 Validation check 2

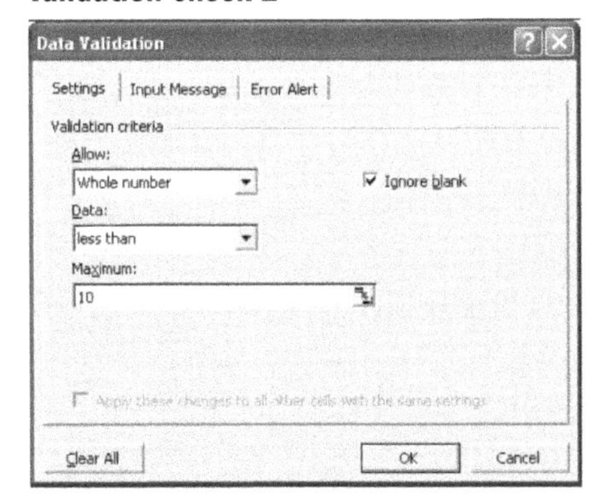

Name of validation check ______________________________

Explanation ______________________________

____

Worksheet 7.1 (continued)

3 Validation check 3

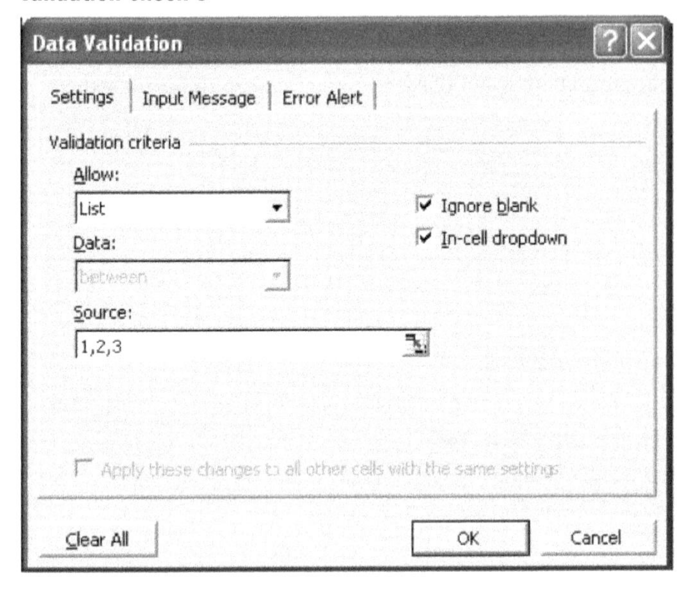

Name of validation check ____

Explanation ____

____

4 Validation check 4

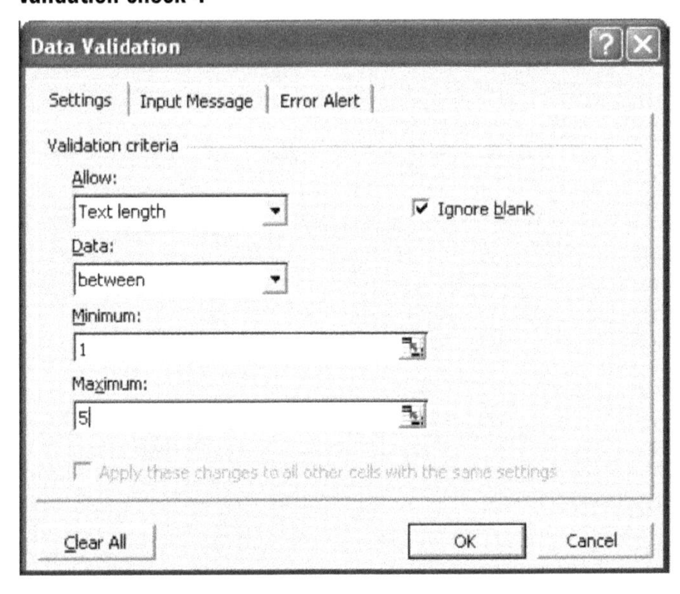

Name of validation check ____

Explanation ____

____

Worksheet 7.1 (continued)

5 Validation check 5

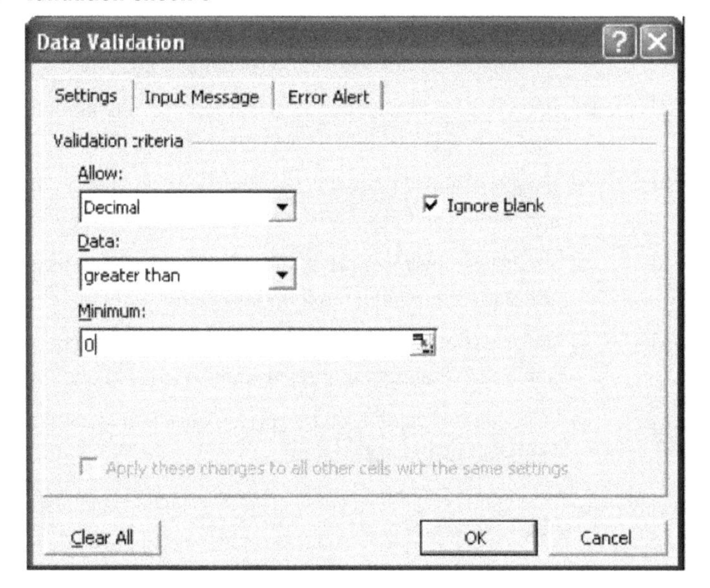

Name of validation check ____

Explanation ____

____

Topic 7 answers

Questions A

Student book page 85

1 a Three marks allocated as follows:

An extra digit added at the end of a long number

That is calculated from all the other numbers

And is used to ensure that the number has been input correctly

b One mark for each example to a maximum of two marks such as:

ISBN (International Standard Book Number)

Barcode/article number on items in a supermarket

Bank account number

Utility (gas, electricity, water, phone) customer number

Part number

2 a One mark for: 12/01/3010 cannot be possible as 3010 is in the future

b One mark for: 01/13/2000 cannot be possible as a British DOB as the max number you can have for the month is 12.

c One mark for: 30/02/1999 is not possible as there is no 30th of February

3 a One mark for an appropriate check and one mark for the reason.

Format check – only allows the letters and numbers in the format chosen

Length check – checks that the code contains exactly 9 characters

b One mark for an appropriate check and one mark for the reason.

Range check – to ensure the salary is within a certain range, e.g. greater than 0 but less than a certain salary

Data type check – to ensure that currency/number has been entered

4 One mark for three points similar to the following:

The data might pass all the validation rules but may still be wrong because the data is allowable and an error is not detected. For example, a date of birth might be 01/12/98 and is typed incorrectly as 12/01/98 which is still a valid date.

5 a One mark for each point to a maximum of three marks. Answers marked in the following way:

Some fields are compulsory such as everyone has a name.

Other fields can be left empty such as email address as not everyone has one.

b One mark for suitable field for a presence check, e.g. name, address, date of birth, etc.

One mark for a suitable field where a presence check would be inappropriate, such as email address, mobile phone number, works phone number, etc.

6 One mark for the name of the method and one mark for a brief description × 3.

Questionnaires in order to ask questions about the old system and the desired new system

Interviews where people at the different levels are asked about their requirements from a system

Observation where the investigator sits in with someone to watch how the existing system works and learn about it

Inspection of records where you look at the documentation produced by the old system

Questions B

Student book page 88

1 One mark each for items in their correct place in the order. Correct order is:

Analysis

Design

Development and testing

Implementation

Documentation

Evaluation

2 a One mark for Design

b One mark for Design

c One mark for Analysis

d One mark for Evaluation

e One mark for Development and testing

3 a One mark for each of two points similar to the following:

Stop using the old system one day and start using the new system the next day.

b One mark for one advantage such as:

It requires fewer resources (people, money and equipment).

One mark for one disadvantage such as:

There is a risk that the new system may not work as expected.

People may not be properly trained to cope with the new system.

Test yourself

Student book page 89

A facts
B input
C implementation
D normal
E whole
F direct changeover
G direct changeover
H parallel running
I training
J documented
K evaluation

Revision questions

Student book page 89

1 One mark for each point up to a maximum of three marks.

Format check so date is entered in the form dd/mm/yy

Presence check to check that data has been entered

Range check to check that the number of days does not go past maximum for the month

Range check to check that a date of birth is not after today's date

2 **a** One mark for 21059810J

b One mark for each point to a maximum of two marks such as:

A check performed by a computer program

To restrict the data being entered

So that it is allowable and reasonable

So that it obeys certain rules before it is accepted

c One mark for each of two methods. Examples include:

Range check: Check that the whole number lies between 1 and 99999999.

Check that the day part lies in the range for acceptable dates, e.g. not 31/02/10 which is impossible.

Check that the year of joining is not before the fitness club opened.

Format check: Check to ensure that exactly 9 characters have been entered.

Check to ensure that the first 8 characters are letters and the last character is a number.

3 One mark for the name and one mark for an advantage × 3.

Direct changeover – requires fewer resources (people, money, equipment) and is simple provided nothing goes wrong.

Parallel running – you still have the old system to rely on if things go wrong.

Phased implementation – IT staff can deal with problems caused by a module before moving on to new modules.

Pilot running – the implementation is on a much smaller and more manageable scale.

Exam-style questions

Student book page 90

1 One mark each for any three from the following:

Direct changeover

Parallel running

Phased implementation

Pilot running

2 One mark each for four of the following:

Validation routines

List of variables

Program flowcharts

Program coding

File structures

System flowcharts

3 **a** Analysis

Design

Development and testing

Implementation

Documentation

Evaluation

b **(i)** Analysis

(ii) Design

(iii) Implementation

(iv) Development and testing

(v) Analysis

(vi) Analysis

4 **a** Two marks for the following:

The hardware and software required to run the system – e.g. type of processor, operating system etc.

How to log in and log out of the system – so users can use the system.

b Two marks for the following:

Program listings/program code – so that the code can be modified.

Meanings of error messages – so that the errors can be corrected.

5 One mark for each correct answer.

	Normal	Abnormal	Extreme
25			√
eighteen		√	
15	√		
30		√	
−5		√	
0			√
10	√		

6 One mark for each correct answer.

	Analysis	Evaluation
Carrying out research on the current system	√	
Comparing the solution with the original task requirements		√
Producing a system specification	√	
Identifying any limitations of the solution		√
Justifying suitable hardware and software for the new system	√	

7 Marks are allocated as follows:

One mark for appropriate spacing for each field

One mark for a forward/backward button

One mark for a save/submit button

One mark each for each of the following fields up to a maximum of seven marks:

Title of book

Author's name

ISBN

Fiction/Non-fiction

Genre (e.g. crime, drama, etc.)

Publisher

Dewey decimal number

Picture of the cover

Cost of book

Hardback/Paperback

Number of pages

8 **a** Three marks for the following:

Conducting interviews to find our how the system works and what improvements are needed.

Using questionnaires to give to users to ask about the existing system including how it works and any problems with it.

Examination of existing documentation to look at reports, input forms etc.

b Two marks for the following:

The efficiency of the new system. For example, an assessment of how well it works and how satisfied users are with it.

The ease of use. For example, how well users are satisfied with the new user interface and how satisfied management are with the information the system gives them.

c Three marks for the following:

Comparing the new system with the initial requirements to see how closely they are met.

Comparing the performance of the new system with that of the old system.

Evaluating user responses to the new system.

d Three marks for the following:

The user interface may need modification to satisfy users.

Bugs or poor performance of the system may need correcting.

9 Six marks for an answer such as the following:

Normal data is data that should pass the validation check. Numbers in the range 150 to 800 inclusive is normal data for this system.

Abnormal data is data that would not pass the validation check. Numbers greater than 800 or less than 150 would be abnormal data.

Extreme data is data on the borderline of that accepted by the system. 150 and 800 are examples of extreme data.

10 Two marks for each matched pair × 2.

Normal data – any item of data between but not including \$100 and \$500

Abnormal data – item of data which does not lie between \$100 and \$500 inclusive, for example \$600

Extreme data – items of data at the extremes of the allowable values so \$100 and \$500 in this case

Worksheet 7.1: Spreadsheet cell validation checks

Teacher resource pack page 65

1 Name of validation check: Range check

Explanation: Only allows the user to enter whole numbers between and including 0 and 15.

2 Name of validation check: Range check

Explanation: Only allows the user to enter a whole number less than 10.

3 Name of validation check: Restricting the user to a list

Explanation: Only allows the user to choose a value of 1, 2 or 3 from a drop-down list.

4 Name of validation check: Format check

Explanation: Only allows from one character to five characters inclusive to be entered.

5 Name of validation check: Range check

Explanation: Allows any number above zero to be entered.

Safety and security

This worksheet can be best used following study of safety and security on pages 92 to 99 of Chapter 8 in the Student Book.

Worksheet 8.1

Can you work out what the word is?

Here are some words or phrases which have been jumbled up. The words are connected with safety and security. Can you work out what they are?
There is a clue to help you.

1 electronic out

Hint: There is the danger of this if you spill a drink over your computer.

Answer: ______________________________

2 print pig

Hint: Wires laid over the floor present this sort of hazard.

Answer: ______________________________

3 adore loved

Hint: You must make sure that sockets are not this.

Answer: ______________________________

4 vote hear

Hint: Ventilation fans covered up can cause computer equipment to do this.

Answer: ______________________________

5 shh in pig

Hint: Using fake emails to get people to reveal their personal details.

Answer: ______________________________

6 prim hang

Hint: Uses programming code to direct users to a fake website with the view of stealing their personal details.

Answer: ______________________________

Worksheet 8.1 (continued)

7 orbit mice

Hint: Authentication method that makes use of a property of the human body.

Answer: ______________________________

8 amps

Hint: Unwanted email.

Answer: ______________________________

9 fierce attic

Hint: A digital one of these is used to authenticate the sender of email.

Answer: ______________________________

10 try in ponce

Hint: Scrambling data before it is sent over the internet.

Answer: ______________________________

Topic 8 answers

Questions A

Student book page 93

1 One mark for each correctly placed tick.

	Health	Safety
Backache caused by incorrect posture whilst using a computer	√	
Overloaded multi-sockets being used		√
Tripping over a trailing wire		√
RSI caused by using a mouse for long periods	√	
Electric shock caused by spilling a drink over a computer		√
Headaches caused by glare on the screen	√	
Eye strain caused by looking at the computer screen for long periods	√	

2 a One mark for one of the following:

Sink wires into floors/lay under floor covering.

Use wireless for data cables.

b One mark for one of the following:

Do not tamper with faulty equipment.

Do not have drinks that can be spilt near the computer equipment.

c One mark for one of the following:

Do not overload sockets.

Remove faulty equipment immediately from use.

d One mark for one of the following:

Ensure that there is enough room on the desk to position equipment properly.

Do not balance equipment.

3 a One mark for: A health risk is some action that you take when using a computer that can damage your health.

One mark for: A safety risk is the risk of an accident when using computer equipment.

b One mark for the risk and one mark for how to prevent the risk × 2

Tripping – Sink wires into floors/lay under floor covering.

Electrocution – Do not tamper with faulty equipment.

Fire – Do not overload power sockets.

Questions B

Student book page 97

1 a One mark for unwanted unsolicited email sent in bulk

b One mark for each annoyance up to a maximum of two marks:

It blocks up your inbox

Slows down your computer

It takes time deleting it

It can take time checking that there is no important email that has been trapped by the spam filter

c One mark for one of the following:

Use software called an anti-spam filter.

Do not readily give your email address out on sites such as blogs and forums.

d One mark each for two of the following:

It will have an unfamiliar email address.

Often the email address contains lots of strings of characters before the @ symbol.

There are often grammar and spelling mistakes in the text of the email.

A proper email will address you by your name.

2 One mark for each correctly placed tick.

	True	False
Unsolicited email is called spam.	√	
Pharming uses SMS to collect card details.		√
Pharming uses programming code which has been put on the user's computer without their knowledge.	√	
Spam is fake messages trying to steal your personal details.		√

3 One mark for each way up to a maximum of five marks.

Authentication using usernames and passwords. The username is used to identify the user to the network and the password is to ensure that only authorised users are given access to the network.

Digital signatures to ensure that emails are authentic.

Authentication using biometric methods such as retinal scanning, iris scanning, fingerprinting or face recognition. Uses a unique property of the human body to identify a person to an ICT system.

4 a Two marks for an answer similar to the following.

E-safety is concerned with using the internet in a safe and responsible way by taking precautions when using the internet.

b One mark for each of four actions such as:

Never arrange to meet an online 'friend' on your own – always take a responsible adult with you.

Never reveal personal information such as your name, address, school name, photograph or any other information from which you can be identified.

Use only websites that are recommended by teachers or your parents.

Do not open an email from an unknown person.

Do not open attachments to emails from people you do not know.

Only send emails to people you know.

Do not use your real name when playing games online.

Use a search engine which has a parental guidance setting which your parents can set so that it filters out any unsuitable content.

Do not email a picture of yourself in school uniform or give the name of your school out.

Know how to block and report unwanted users in chat rooms.

5 a One mark for a definition such as - a discussion on the internet where people can join the discussion and add their comments

b i One mark for - an unmoderated forum does not have a moderator controlling the content so users can post whatever they want.

One mark for - a moderated forum is controlled by a moderator who checks the comments before posting them.

ii One mark for - in an unmoderated forum people can post rude and offensive messages.

One mark for - in a moderated forum if people posted rude or offensive messages then these could be checked and removed by the moderator if found unacceptable.

Questions C

Student book page 99

1 a Two marks for:

A program that replicates itself automatically and can do harm by copying files, deleting files or corrupting files

b One mark each for three steps such as:

Install antivirus software.

Keep the antivirus software up-to-date.

Do not open file attachments sent from people you do not know.

Do not download software from file-sharing sites.

2 a Two marks for:

Accessing a computer system without permission

b Three marks for three steps such as:

Change passwords regularly.

Install antispyware software on your computer.

Do not write usernames or passwords down.

Use long passwords containing upper and lower case characters with numbers and symbols to make them harder to crack.

Do not divulge passwords to anyone who asks for them.

Watch out for 'shoulder surfers' when entering passwords.

3 One mark for each correct answer.

	True	False
Email attachments can contain viruses.	True	
Viruses consist of programming code designed to cause harm or annoyance to your computer.	True	
It is impossible to hack into a computer without using the internet.		False
Antivirus software must be kept up-to-date.	True	

4 a One mark for antivirus software

b One mark each for two actions such as:

Do not open file attachments from people you do not know.

Do not download software from file-sharing sites.

5 a Two points for two marks.

Storage in the cloud is a way of storing data in one place so that it can be accessed by all your devices as long as you have internet access. Basically, you store your files on a file server in a remote place (called the cloud) and you access your files using a user-ID and password.

b One mark for:

All your data is in one place which you can access via any device as long as it has internet access.

c One mark for each point up to a maximum of four marks.

The company providing the storage could go out of business. If this happens then you have to consider what would happen to your data.

Some of the data could be personal data, in which case it should be encrypted so that if it is hacked into by hackers, they would not be able to understand and use the data.

You have to trust that the organisation providing the storage puts in place all the security measures to keep your data safe.

Who owns the data when it is stored in a cloud? When photographs are stored using some cloud storage organisations, you have to give permission that anyone can access and use the photographs you store.

Test yourself

Student book page 100

A firewall
B antivirus
C files
D download
E hacking
F phishing
G spam filters
H pharming, fake
I encrypted, hackers
J passwords, biometric
K digital signatures

Revision questions

Student book page 101

1 a One mark for a definition similar to the following.

Storage in the cloud is a way of storing data in one place so that it can be accessed by all your devices as long as you have internet access.

b One mark for one advantage such as:

You can access your data from any device that has internet access.

You do not have to worry about backing up your data as you can synchronise your files so that any data you store on your hard disk is also stored on the cloud.

One mark for one disadvantage such as:

The organisation storing the data could go out of business.

You do not have control of the security of the data.

You may lose the copyright of photographs stored.

2 One mark for each correctly placed tick.

	Smishing	Phishing	Pharming
Uses emails		√	
Involves fake programming code being loaded onto a computer			√
Does not involve being directed to a website		√	
Uses SMS messages	√		

3 One mark for each correctly placed tick.

	True	False
Tripping accidents can be caused by trailing wires.	√	
It is safe to use lots of multi-sockets connected to the one plug.		√
Overloaded power sockets can cause fires.	√	
Wastepaper bins should be emptied regularly to reduce the fire risk.	√	

4 a One mark for each of three methods:

Use a firewall to prevent hackers.

Protect access using a system of usernames and passwords.

Advise users to change passwords regularly.

Use passwords which are long and contain upper and lower case characters including numbers and symbols.

b One mark for each of three things such as:

Do not allow students to use removable media.

Install antivirus software.

Keep the antivirus software up-to-date.

Do not allow students to download programs or games.

5 a i One mark for: secure socket layer

ii One mark for: creates an encrypted link between two computers which will prevent hackers from using the data if intercepted

b One mark for: the web address starts with https

6 One mark for each of three points from the following:

Do not open emails from unknown sources.

Do not open file attachments to emails from people you do not know.

Do not reply to any email asking for personal details such as credit card details or passwords.

7 One mark for each method up to a maximum of three marks.

Use SSL (Secure Socket Layer).

Check that the website address starts with https.

Use an encrypted link.

Do not follow a link to the bank site.

Exam-style questions

Student book page 102

1 One mark for each answer similar to the following:

a Pharming – installing malicious code in a person's computer which directs them to a fake site which looks like a banking site and then gets them to reveal personal details

b Phishing – Using fake emails pretending to be from the target's bank to get them to reveal banking/personal details

2 One mark for an explanation of spam similar to the following:

Spam – unwanted/unasked for email/junk email

One mark for an example such as:

It wastes time having to read and delete it.

It takes up storage space before deletion.

3 a One mark for each of two health issues such as:

Headaches caused by prolonged computer use

RSI through typing for prolonged periods

Back problems caused by bad posture

b One mark for each of two safety issues such as:

Trailing wires in a computer room

Too many plugs in an electric socket

Drinking whilst using a computer

4 One mark for each correct answer.

	Pharming	Phishing
Malicious programming code is stored on a computer.	√	
Emails are sent pretending to be from your bank.		√
You are redirected to a bogus/fake website.	√	
Uses emails for identity theft.		√

5 a Two marks for an answer such as the following:

E-safety is concerned with using the internet in a safe and responsible way by taking precautions such as not divulging personal details when using the internet

b One mark for each point up to a maximum of five marks.

There is an unpleasant/dangerous side to the internet.

You have to protect yourself from accidental or physical harm.

People can hide their identity when using the internet.

People may not be genuine – they may not be who they say they are.

Some bad people will use the internet to look for their next victim.

You could end up being stalked.

People can tell lies about you and post them online.

People can steal your identity if you disclose your personal information.

6 One mark each for three precautions such as:

Never arrange to meet an online 'friend' on your own – always take a responsible adult with you.

Never reveal personal information such as your name, address, school name, photograph or any other information from which you can be identified.

Use only websites that are recommended by teachers or your parents.

Do not open an email from an unknown person.

Do not open attachments to emails from people you do not know.

Only send emails to people you know.

Do not use your real name when playing games online.

Use a search engine which has a parental guidance setting which your parents can set so that it filters out any unsuitable content.

Do not email a picture of yourself in school uniform or give the name of your school out.

Know how to block and report unwanted users in chat rooms.

7 a One mark for three answers similar to the following:

They may alter/delete accounts.

They may alter the data in the accounts (e.g. add money to them).

They may use personal information to create new fictitious accounts.

They may transfer money to the hacker's account.

b One mark each for three of the following:

Usernames and passwords – usernames identify the user to the system and passwords ensure that only the correct user is using the account.

Biometrics – uses a unique property of a person (e.g. fingerprints, retina/iris pattern) in order to authenticate a user.

Use of a card with a chip – uses a password so only if the password was known and the person had the card would they be allowed access.

8 One mark each for three of the following:

Prevents the computer from accessing undesirable sites and content

Prevents unauthorised computers gaining access using the internet and thus helps prevent hackers from accessing the data

Warns you an unauthorised computer is trying to log onto your network

Keeps lists of undesirable sites that your computer should not be allowed access to

9 One mark for each correct answer:

a Encrypting

b Spamming

c Phishing

d Pharming

e Smishing

f Encrypting

10 One mark for each point up to a maximum of four points.

Set privacy settings so that only people you know can contact you.

Do not accept friend requests from people you do not know.

Use appropriate language.

Never arrange to meet strangers you have chatted to online.

Do not share personal information or images with people you do not know.

Do not post other people's personal addresses or phone numbers.

Tell a responsible adult if something concerns or worries you.

Do not click on suspicious links on social media.

11 One mark for each point to a maximum of three marks.

Checking to ensure there are no trailing wires that could cause a tripping hazard

Ensuring that you and others do not drink near computers and risk electric shocks/electrocution

Checking that cooling vents on computers, printers, etc., are not covered by paper, clothing, etc., which could cause overheating with the possibility of fires

Ensure that any faulty equipment is removed immediately from use

Making sure that too many plugs are not plugged into a multi-socket which could cause overloading and a fire hazard

Taking regular breaks so that you do not risk some of the health problems associated with using computers for lengthy periods without breaks such as eye strain, back ache and RSI (Repetitive Strain Injury)

Assessing the ergonomic way you are working by checking you comply with all the health and safety regulations and advice about chairs, screens, seating position, lighting, etc.

12 a Two marks for:

Data about a living identifiable person (1) such as their date of birth, banking details, religion, etc. (1)

b One mark each for two of the following:

Own name, address, school name, picture of yourself in school uniform, etc.

c Two reasons, one mark each, such as:

To keep yourself safe from physical harm

To ensure you are not bullied or stalked

To ensure you are not exposed to offensive or violent images

To ensure you are not tricked into committing a crime

13 One mark for each correct line.

	True	False
Firewalls prevent people from inside and outside the organisation accessing a computer/network.		✓
Anti-virus software will detect all viruses.		✓
It is impossible for hackers to understand encrypted data.		✓

14 There are a huge number of valid reasons, so any two valid reasons (one mark each) such as:

There is a huge amount of material on every subject imaginable.

You can access the information from any device that has internet access.

The use of search engines means that specific information can be found quickly.

15 a One mark for each correct advantage up to a maximum of four:

There is a larger amount of storage available on the cloud.

He does not have to worry about backing up his data as the people who set up the cloud take the responsibility of backup.

An SSD is small and is easily lost/stolen.

An SSD can be damaged.

The same file can be accessed by anyone who has the permissions.

Data on the cloud can be accessed from any device connected to the internet.

Storage in small amounts is free where you would have to pay for the SSD.

b One mark for each correct disadvantage up to a maximum of three:

If you have a large amount of storage then you need to commit to a monthly/annual charge.

Anyone who has your username and password could access your data.

The organisation supplying the cloud storage could go out of business.

You are trusting an outside organisation to store your data securely.

Internet access is needed to access the files.

A stable internet connection is required as data is constantly being saved automatically to the cloud.

16 One mark for a correct explanation:

Using an additional method of authentication to the usual user-ID and password combination

Two marks for descriptions of two correct methods:

Sending a security code to your phone which you type in to ensure it is you accessing the information/placing an order

Using a biometric method such as fingerprint or iris recognition as an additional authentication method

Worksheet 8.1: Can you work out what the word is?

Teacher resource pack page 72

1. Electrocution
2. Tripping
3. Overloaded
4. Overheat
5. Phishing
6. Pharming
7. Biometric
8. Spam
9. Certificate
10. Encryption

Audience

This activity can be best used following study of copyright and software piracy on pages 104 and 105 of Chapter 9 in the Student Book.

Activity 9.1 The legal, moral and ethical implications of software piracy

In this activity, you have to create a poster which is to be put up on a wall in a school/college computer room. The aim of the poster is to make computer users aware of the legal, moral and ethical implications of software piracy.

You should do some research on the topic first using the internet and combine this information with what you already know from your textbook or lesson notes.

Many people do not think about the problems caused by software piracy as they usually only think of it in terms of themselves being able to obtain the software cheaply or even for free.

Hence, you need to make your poster hard hitting.

Feel free to use your imagination.

The poster can be created using any suitable software and should be designed using an A4-sized page.

There are many sites that you can visit to get some content and hopefully some ideas. For example visit the sites for the BBC, *The Guardian* and Software.org/BSA Foundation, and search for 'online piracy'.

Topic 9 answers

Test yourself

Student book page 106

A audience

B needs

C piracy

D legislation

E money

F viruses

G dongle

H encrypt

I digital

Revision questions

Student book page 106

1 Two marks for:

The illegal copying of computer software that is protected by copyright

2 One mark each for two of the following:

To make sure that your solution addresses these needs

To make it appropriate for the age of the audience

To make it appropriate for their level of literacy

To tailor the solution to how much they know about the subject

3 One mark for each correctly placed tick.

	TRUE	FALSE
The illegal copying of computer software is an example of software piracy.	√	
Copying software is always illegal.		√
Software piracy is acceptable as it helps us obtain software cheaper or for free.		√
Software licences usually allow you to run a certain number of computers with the same software.	√	
Copying deprives small software producers of money.	√	

Exam-style questions

Student book page 106

1 a Two marks for an answer similar to the following:

It protects software authors who have invested time and money into developing the software from having their work illegally copied, thus depriving them of income.

b i One mark for one of the following:

To make a copy of the software for backup purposes in case the original was damaged or lost

Where the software licence allows it to be copied

ii One mark each for two of the following:

What exactly illegal copying is

The penalty for illegal copying

2 One mark for each point up to a maximum of four marks.

The audience is young so plenty of colour is needed to attract young children.

Use of animation and cartoon characters will help keep them engaged.

The audience is trying to learn to read so simple activities for them to try would be needed.

A child will learn better if a game can be created which helps them learn.

3 a One mark for the illegal copying of software or the copying of software that is not allowed by the software licence

b One mark for an answer similar to:

Illegal copying deprives the copyright owner of income so they need to be protected

c One mark each for two brief descriptions of methods such as:

Encryption of the execution code – the execution code enables the software to run. This code is encrypted and a key is needed to unlock the code to enable the software to be used.

Use of a digital signature on the DVD/CD containing the software – this prevents the software being copied exactly.

Use of an activation key – when you purchase software, after loading it on your computer, you will be asked to activate the software by going onto the software producer's website and then entering a product activation key (a long code).

Use of a dongle – a dongle is a piece of hardware that attaches to a computer using the USB port and allows a secured piece of software to run.

Use of programming code – the program code can be altered to help block copying.

Use of guards – guards are hardware or software modules that keep a check of the program as it is being run to check that it has not been tampered with in any way.

Communication

This worksheet can be best used following study of communication using ICT on pages 107 to 111 of Chapter 10 in the Student Book.

Worksheet 10.1

Can you work out what the word is?

Match the clues on this page with the list of words on the next page. Write the correct letter next to each clue. All the words are connected with email communication.

1 An electronic message ☐

2 If you are sending the same email to more than one person, you are sending to a ________________ ☐

3 A file sent with an email ☐

4 An email sent to you which you send on to others ☐

5 Where you keep your list of contact addresses ☐

6 You must not use this kind of language in emails ☐

7 Copy of an email sent to others for their information ☐

8 Method of keeping emails private ☐

9 Unwanted email that you waste time deleting ☐

10 Emails are checked for these by your virus checker ☐

A	Forward
B	Carbon copy
C	Spam
D	File attachment
E	Email
F	Address book
G	Viruses
H	Group
I	Encryption
J	Abusive

This worksheet can be best used following study of the section on evaluating information on the internet on page 111 of Chapter 10, in the Student Book.

Worksheet 10.2

Creating an evaluation checklist for websites

You have been asked to evaluate a website. Think about the sorts of things you look for in a good website.

Produce a checklist consisting of 20 things you should look for in a good website.

1 ....

....

2 ....

....

3 ....

....

4 ....

....

5 ....

....

6 ....

....

7 ....

....

8 ....

....

9 ....

....

10 ....

....

11 ....

....

12 ....

....

Worksheet 10.2 (continued)

13 ....

....

14 ....

....

15 ....

....

16 ....

....

17 ....

....

18 ....

....

19 ....

....

20 ....

....

This worksheet can be best used following study of social networking sites on page 111 of Chapter 10 in the Student Book.

Worksheet 10.3

Social media terms – how well do you know them?

There has been a huge increase in the use of social networking and web log sites over the last few years. There are a number of terms which are associated with social networking and web logs. Many of these terms are now so popular you can find them in the latest dictionaries. How many do you know? If you are unsure, have a guess - you will probably be right.

Write your definition or meaning in the space provided.

1 Finsta

Meaning: ______________________________

____

____

2 #Ad/Spon

Meaning: ______________________________

____

____

3 Vlogger

Meaning: ______________________________

____

____

4 Tag

Meaning: ______________________________

____

____

5 Ghosting

Meaning: ______________________________

____

____

Worksheet 10.3 (continued)

6 Cancelled

Meaning: ______________________________

____

____

7 Dragging site

Meaning: ______________________________

____

____

8 Analytics

Meaning: ______________________________

____

____

9 Grid post

Meaning: ______________________________

____

____

This activity can be best used following study of evaluating information on the internet on page 111 of Chapter 10 in the Student Book.

Activity 10.1

The hidden dangers in using the internet

Many older people use the internet without realising the dangers. They do not realise there are many people around who prey on people who are not wary or suspicious of messages, phone calls, emails, and links.

You have been asked to produce a leaflet to hand out to older members of the community warning them of the dangers when using the internet.

Make sure you outline the following in your leaflet:

- Hacking
- Card cloning
- Phishing
- Pharming
- Smishing
- Vishing

You should also include a list of things they can do to prevent them becoming a victim of internet fraudsters.

Activity 10.2

Explaining the features of email

For this activity you have to explain some of the features of email using a screenshot.

A screenshot is a picture of the screen you are looking at. To take a screenshot of the screen you are looking at you press the 'Prt Scr' key on the keyboard. To take a screenshot of the currently selected window, hold down the 'Alt' key and press 'Prt Scr'.

A copy of the entire screen is held in the clipboard and this allows you to paste it into a document like this.

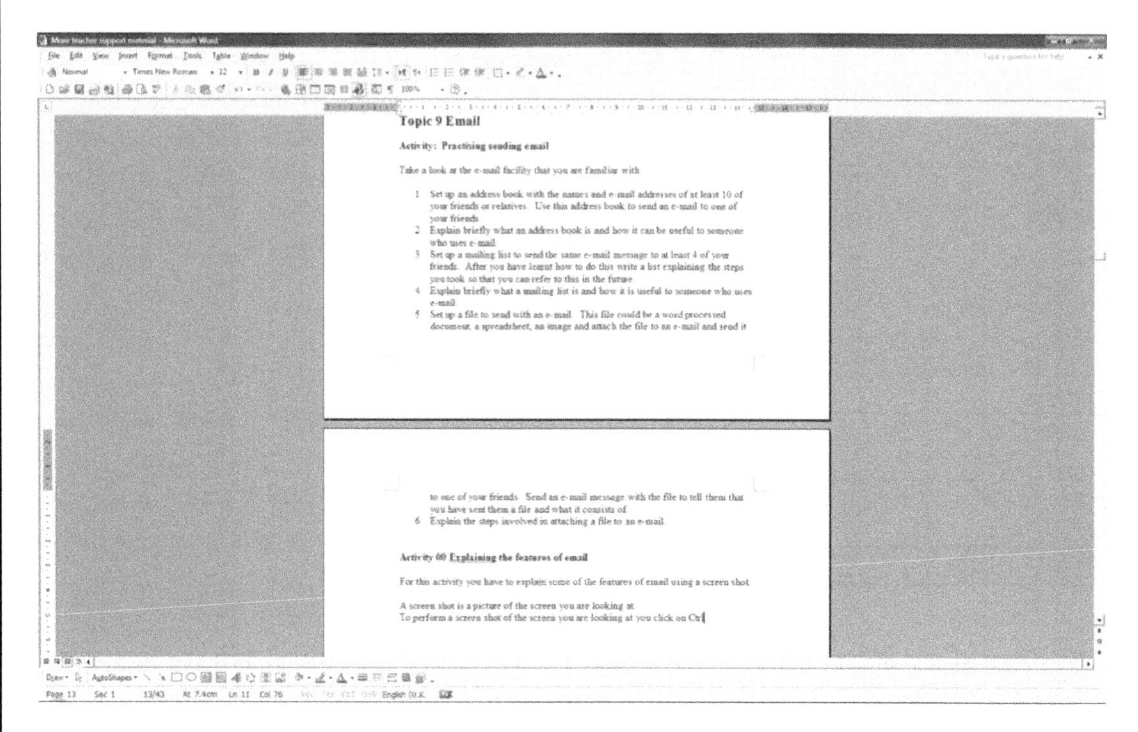
Topic 9 Email

Activity: Practising sending email

Take a look at the e-mail facility that you are familiar with.

1 Set up an address book with the names and e-mail addresses of at least 10 of your friends or relatives. Use this address book to send an e-mail to one of your friends.
2 Explain briefly what an address book is and how it can be useful to someone who uses e-mail.
3 Set up a mailing list to send the same e-mail message to at least 4 of your friends. After you have learnt how to do this write a list explaining the steps you took so that you can refer to this in the future.
4 Explain briefly what a mailing list is and how it is useful to someone who uses e-mail.
5 Set up a file to send with an e-mail. This file could be a word processed document, a spreadsheet, an image and attach the file to an e-mail and send it to one of your friends. Send an e-mail message with the file to tell them that you have sent them a file and what it consists of.
6 Explain the steps involved in attaching a file to an e-mail.

Activity 00 Explaining the features of email

For this activity you have to explain some of the features of email using a screen shot.

A screen shot is a picture of the screen you are looking at.
To perform a screen shot of the screen you are looking at you click on Ctrl

You have to do this for the opening screen of the email package you use.

You now have to paste this into a word-processed document.

When you have done this, you need to explain the various parts/features of the email package by making use of arrows and text boxes. This process is called annotation.

When you have completed this work, save a copy and print the work out to show to your teacher/lecturer.

Topic 10 answers

Test yourself

Student book page 112

A internet, accessing

B HTTP

C HTTPS, encrypt

D locator

E hyperlink

F ISP

G blog, blogger

H domain

I web browser, search engine

Revision questions

Student book page 112

1 One mark for each correctly placed tick.

	True	False
An intranet is a type of blog.		√
Intranets are used by people within an organisation.	√	
Intranets and the internet both use similar technology.	√	
An ISP is a type of virus.		√

2 One mark each for two features such as:

Uses external links

Usually has just one author

Entries are usually in reverse chronological order

Usually personal

Readers can add comments but are unable to edit the blog

3 One mark for each similarity or difference up to a maximum of four marks.

Similarities:

Both use internet technology.

The internet is a network of networks whereas an intranet is a single network.

Differences:

An intranet is a private network whereas the internet is a public network.

Intranet access is restricted to a particular organisation and their trading partners.

4 One mark for each point to a maximum of four marks.

A wiki is a web page that can be viewed and modified by anyone who has a web browser. This means people can alter the content of the web pages. The encyclopaedia Wikipedia is an example of a wiki.

5 One mark for each correct answer.

	True	False
Spam is unsolicited email.	√	
Email groups are used to avoid spam.		√
Email groups are useful for when the same email needs to be sent to all members of the group.	√	
Spam filters can remove harmful viruses.		√
Storage in the cloud is useful if you need to access the data using lots of different devices.	√	

6 One mark for each point up to a maximum of four marks.

A web browser is a piece of software used to view web pages written in HTML code. A search engine is software used to search for specific information on the internet by using search criteria.

Exam-style questions

Student book page 113

1 Two marks for:

The internet is a network of networks.

The World Wide Web is a means of accessing information contained on the internet.

2 **a** Two marks for an answer similar to the following:

An intranet is a network which uses the same technology as the internet.

b One mark for one way such as:

It is confined to a single organisation and their trading partners.

There is no general access to the public.

It is a much smaller network.

3 One mark for each correctly placed tick.

Use of chip and PIN	
Registration system that makes use of a registration code	√
The use of antivirus software	
Encryption of the programming code used to execute the program	√
Use of data protection legislation	
Use of activation codes which can only be used a certain number of times on different machines	√
The use of a dongle	√

4 One mark for the name and one mark for a brief description × 2.

Encryption of the execution code – the execution code enables the software to run. This code is encrypted and a key is needed to unlock the code to enable the software to be used.

Use of a digital signature on the DVD/CD containing the software – this prevents the software being copied exactly.

Use of an activation key – when you purchase software, after loading it on your computer, you will be asked to activate the software by going onto the software producer's website and then entering a product activation key (a long code).

Use of a dongle – a dongle is a piece of hardware that attaches to a computer using the USB port and allows a secured piece of software to run. The dongle contains an electronic key that unlocks the program on the computer and allows it to run. Making a copy of the dongle is hard.

Use of programming code – the program code can be altered to help block copying.

Use of guards – guards are hardware or software modules that keep a check of the program as it is being run to ensure that it has not been tampered with in any way.

5 One mark each for three features such as:

You create your profile containing information about yourself such as interests, hobbies, etc.

Other people with similar interests can get in touch

Members of the site can communicate using email, blogs, instant messaging, etc.

You can invite people into your circle of friends.

You can post photographs and limit access to them to certain people.

6 **a** One mark for each of three advantages such as:

It is much faster to find relevant information compared to looking in books.

The information is more likely to be up-to-date compared to books.

The information may use multimedia which can make it easier to understand.

It is easier to compare different sources of information to verify the accuracy of the information.

b One mark for each of three disadvantages such as:

Anyone can create a website and post information without checking it.

This means that some of the information may be incorrect.

Some websites are set up deliberately to mislead you.

The information will not be as reliable as information in books as books are usually written by experts.

7 One mark for each correct answer.

	True	False
The internet is a network of networks.	√	
Intranets can be used by anyone with internet access.		√
Intranets and the internet both use web browsers.	√	
The internet uses HTTP.	√	

8 One mark each for three differences similar to the following:

A blog has a single author but a wiki has many authors.

A blog is written in reverse chronological order but a wiki can have any order since it is determined by the users and the content they post.

Users cannot edit a blog, they can only add their comments, whereas a Wiki can be edited.

A blog is usually personal (i.e. about a particular person) whereas a wiki can be about anything.

9 **a** Intranet

b Intranet

c Internet

d Intranet

10 One mark for each point up to a maximum of six marks.

A blog is public so anyone can see it whereas with social media you can choose who can see the information (e.g. usually your friends). Viewers can only add their comments to a blog but they cannot alter what the author of the blog has written as the blog is written by just one author. The aim of social networking is to keep in touch with a group of friends and let them know what you are doing. It is easy to arrange meetings using social networking and you can get replies back from messages sent very quickly. Many people regard social networking sites as bad because it can lead to seclusion. There is also the danger of stalking and bullying on social networking sites.

11 One mark for each of three points such as:

Data/files are not stored locally on disk, pen drive, etc.

They are stored on servers in remote locations.

Can be saved and accessed by making use of the internet.

You can access the files using any device provided it has internet access.

Worksheet 10.1: Can you work out what the word is?

Teacher resource pack page 81

1. Email
2. Group
3. File attachment
4. Forward
5. Address book
6. Abusive
7. Carbon copy
8. Encryption
9. Spam
10. Viruses

Worksheet 10.2: Creating an evaluation checklist for websites

Teacher resource pack page 83

Here are some of the many possible criteria:
Is the content of the site accurate?
Is the content easy to understand?
Is the content free from spelling and grammatical errors?
Can you tell when the site was last updated?
Is the content kept up-to-date?
Does the site have a search facility?
Is the site easy to navigate?
Do the pages appear overcrowded?
Has colour been used to good effect?
Have appropriate images been included?
Did the site take a long time to load?
Have any annoying animations been included?
Have suitable fonts and font sizes been included?
Do all the links work?
If the links are followed, do they link to relevant and interesting material?
Have long scrolling pages been avoided?
Are there too many pop-up advertisements on the pages?
Is there any general useful information such as the weather on the page?
Is the information on the page in a sensible order?
Does it tell you how many people have viewed the page (i.e. does it include a counter)?

Worksheet 10.3: Social media terms – how well do you know them?

Teacher resource pack page 85

1. Finsta

   Having two Instagram accounts: a real Instagram account and then a 'fake Insta' which can only be seen by close friends.

2. #Ad/Spon

   A tag which social media influencers are legally required to add to anything they have received for free or have been paid to post about.

3. Vlogger

   A person who posts their comments via a vlog.

4. Tag

   A trend for a video format that goes around YouTube.

5. Ghosting

   Removing a person from your list of friends on a social networking site, often without warning or explanation.

6. Cancelled

   When a social media influencer/celebrity does or says something that ends their career, for example the uncovering of unacceptable tweets they made in the past.

7. Dragging site

   An online forum in which people, often anonymous, make allegations about social media influencers and other people in prominent positions These allegations are often vicious and false.

8. Analytics

   Data that influencers can see about their viewers/followers.

9. Grid post

   The photos on someone's Instagram profile (rather than the photos on their story).

File management

This worksheet can be best used following study of file formats on pages 114 to 116 of Chapter 11 in the Student Book.

Worksheet 11.1

File formats

Can you recognise file formats and know what they are used for?

You have to be familiar with different file formats in the exam. Use your knowledge to fill in the following table. The first row has been filled in for you.

File format	Typical use
.htm	Used for storing web pages
.csv	
.css	
.txt	
.rtf	
.gif	
.pdf	
.jpg	
.zip	

Topic 11 answers

Worksheet 11.1

Teacher resource pack page 92

File format	Typical use
.htm	Used for storing web pages.
.csv	A generic file format used to hold a list of data items that are separated by commas and have a table-type structure
.css	Used for formatting the content of web pages so that it is easy to ensure consistency from one web page to another
.txt	A generic file just containing text without any formatting and used to import text into different software packages
.rtf	Saves text with a limited amount of formatting and used to transfer text from one package to another
.gif	Used for storing graphic images on the web. They load quickly because the file is compressed
.pdf	Used as a format for documents as the software to view the document is widely available and free
.jpg	A file format used by digital cameras to store images. The file format uses compression
.zip	Used to archive files downloaded from the internet. The files are compressed and need to be decompressed before they can be used

Exam-style questions

Student book page 117

1 **a** One mark for:

A file format that can be used by different software no matter who the manufacturer of the software is.

One mark for:

So that they can be loaded by others who may not have the same software as the original file was created in.

b Three marks for: *.txt .csv .pdf*

2 One mark for each situation and one mark for the reason.

To send a file as an attachment to an email where there is a restriction on the size of the attachment that can be sent. Compression reduces the file size and enables the file attachment to be sent.

To reduce the storage space needed to hold large files such as video or photo libraries. Reducing file size will enable more files to be stored.

Images

This worksheet can be best used following study of use of software tools to edit images on pages 118 to 119 of Chapter 12 in the Student Book.

Worksheet 12.1

Understanding terms used when manipulating images

Here are some terms used when dealing with images. The meanings of these terms have become mixed up. Match the correct definition to the term.

Term	Definition
Aspect ratio	The difference between the light and dark parts of an image
Cropping	Making the image smaller or larger
Colour depth	The ratio of the width to the height of an image
Resizing	Flipping an image
Resolution	The number of bits used to represent the colours in an image
Contrast	The sharpness or clarity of an image
Reflecting	Using only part of an image

Topic 12 answers

Teacher resource pack page 94

Worksheet 12.1 Understanding terms used when manipulating images

Term	Meaning
Aspect ratio	The ratio of the width to the height of an image
Cropping	Using only part of an image
Colour depth	The number of bits used to represent the colours in an image
Resizing	Making the image smaller or larger
Resolution	The sharpness or clarity of an image
Contrast	The difference between the light and dark parts of an image
Reflecting	Flipping an image

Layout

This worksheet can be best used following study of organising page layout on page 135 of Chapter 13 in the Student Book.

Worksheet 13.1

Understanding layout

The page layout is the arrangement of items such as text, images and other features on the page. Here are some icons which represent layout options. Your task is to explain what each of these will do to the page layout if you click on them.

Icon/button	What it does to alter the page layout
Columns	
Orientation	
Size	
Breaks	

Topic 13 answers

Teacher resource pack page 96

Worksheet 13.1 Understanding layout

Icon/button	What it does to alter the page layout
Columns	Puts the text into columns. You can also set the width of each column and the space between the columns and even have a vertical line or lines separating the column.
Orientation	Sets the page orientation; it can be portrait or landscape.
Size	Sets the page size of the document, usually to the paper size the printout is to be on (e.g. A4, A0, etc.).
Breaks	Forces the computer to start a new page, rather than allow it to start a page only when the page is completely filled. You also insert section breaks and column breaks so that the text can run on from one section or column to the next.
	Used to adjust the line spacing between lines of text in a document to typically 1.0, 1.15, 1.5, 2.0, 2.5 lines.
	Used to decrease or increase the indent level of a paragraph.
	Aligns the text to both the left and right margins (i.e. fully justify text).

Styles

This worksheet can be best used following study of house style on pages 140 to 142 of Chapter 14 in the Student Book.

Worksheet 14.1

Looking at house style for the NHS (National Health Service)

The NHS (National Health Service) provides free healthcare for the residents of the United Kingdom. The NHS has a house style for all its documents, and all staff producing documents must adhere to this house style. The house style means that all documents have a similar appearance no matter who produced them.

Use the internet to find more guidance on this. Type 'NHS identity stationery' into your browser to locate a very helpful website.

It spells out to anyone who is producing materials how to position items on the page, which font to use, the size of margins, and so on.

After looking at these web pages, answer the following questions:

1 You are going to produce a letter for the NHS. Write down a list of the things you will need to check on the design of the letter.

2 Why is it so important that everyone adheres to the guidelines on this web page?

3 Explain what is meant by house style. Give three examples of house style.

4 **a** Explain where the following would be positioned on the page:

i Header

ii Footer

b Briefly explain the purposes of a header and a footer.

Topic 14 answers

Activity 14.1

Student book page 141

1 Serif
2 Sans serif
3 Sans serif
4 Serif
5 Serif
6 Sans serif
7 Serif
8 Sans serif
9 Serif
10 Sans serif

Worksheet 14.1 answers

Teacher resource pack page 98

1 Here are some of the many things regarding letters which would need to be considered:

The font style – suggests Frutiger as the primary font and Arial as the secondary font should be used for word-processed letters

The size of the font used for key items

The size and position of the logo

The colour used for the logo and the text of key items

Left margin aligned (i.e. not justified)

A blocked format without indented paragraphs

The colour of the paper used

2 So all the letters have a consistent look to reinforce the corporate identity.

So all the letters look the same no matter who in the organisation produced them.

3 A house style means that any document produced by the business should have a similar design although the content can be different. This means all documents produced by the organisation should look similar and do not depend on the person who has produced them.

Any three such as:

- The colours, size and positioning of the logo
- The font or fonts used for headings and main body text
- The font sizes used for the text
- The margins
- Positioning of key items such as the business name and address.

4 **a** **i** A header is text positioned in the margin at the top of a document.

ii A footer is text positioned in the margin at the bottom of a document.

b Headers and footers can be used to hold the following information:

Page numbers

Today's date

The title of the document

A company logo (it can be a graphic image)

The author's name

The file name of the file that is used to hold the document

15 Proofing

Topic 15 answers

Activity 15.1

Student book page 145

All most – should be almost. Not found by spellchecker as 'All' and 'most' are both correctly spelt words.

'posible' should be 'possible' and the spellchecker will detect this.

'acess' should be 'access' and the spellchecker will detect this.

'sceince' should be 'science' and the spellchecker will detect this.

'data' is repeated twice and the spellchecker will detect this.

'transfered' should be 'transferred' and the spellchecker will detect this.

'alowing' should be 'allowing' and the spellchecker will detect this.

Questions A

Student book page 148

1 a One mark for: 12/01/3010 cannot be possible as 3010 is in the future

b One mark for: 01/13/2000 cannot be possible as a British DOB as the max number you can have for the month is 12.

c One mark for: 30/02/1999 is not possible as there is no 30th of February

2 One mark for three points similar to the following:

The data might pass all the validation rules but may still be wrong; however, because the data is allowable an error is not detected. For example, a date of birth might be 01/12/98 and is typed incorrectly as 12/01/98 which is still a valid date.

Revision questions

Student book page 148

1 One mark for each point to a maximum of two marks.

Visual checking/verification

The typed-in data is compared with the original data

2 One mark for each point to a maximum of three marks.

Format check so date is entered in the form dd/mm/yy

Presence check to check that data has been entered

Range check to check that the number of days does not go past that for the month

Range check to check that a date of birth is not after today's date

Exam-style questions

Student book page 148

1 One mark each for a description of the software and then two marks each for two things each piece of software does.

Spellchecker checks words against a stored dictionary and suggests possible changes if the word has been misspelt. Grammar checker checks the construction of the sentences and checks if the rules of grammar are correct. It makes suggestions of changes.

Spellchecker:

- identifies words misspelt as they are typed
- can check an entire document for misspelt words
- offers suggestions as to words the misspelt words could be
- allows you to add words to the spellchecker that are not in its dictionary
- can be used to help you improve your spelling
- checks if the same word has been typed in twice next to each other.

Grammar checker:

- checks that sentences start with a capital letter and end with a full stop
- checks there is only one full stop
- checks that sentences are constructed correctly
- identifies sentences with incorrect grammar by underlining or changing the text colour
- provides explanations of what is wrong and suggestions for improvement.

2 One mark for name of the method and one mark for a description × 2.

Data is entered twice/the double entry of data

Computer compares both versions and only accepts the data if they are the same

Visual checking/verification

The typed-in data is compared with the original data to ensure that the data is the same.

3 Two marks for an answer similar to the following:

a Validation checks are used to restrict the user as to the data they can enter into an ICT system. Verification checks are checks performed to ensure that the data being entered perfectly matches the source of the data.

b One mark each of the following:

i validation check

ii verification check

iii verification check

iv validation check

Graphs and charts

This activity can be best used following study of producing graphs and charts on pages 161 to 164 of Chapter 16 in the Student Book.

Activity 16.1

Producing pie charts

1 Key the data into the spreadsheet as shown in the screenshot.

	A	B	C	D	E
1	**Results of a survey on crisp preferences for two groups in the school**				
2					
3					
4					
5	**Group 7A**	**Number of students**		**Group 9A**	**Number of students**
6	Plain	10		Plain	10
7	Cheese and onion	9		Cheese and onion	10
8	Salt and vinegar	8		Salt and vinegar	3
9	Barbeque beef	4		Barbeque beef	2
10					

Using spreadsheet software, produce two pie charts: one to show Group 7A's and the other to show Group 9A's crisp preferences.

Once you have produced the second pie chart, position it on the screen next to the first pie chart as shown in the following screenshot. You may need to re-size the charts to do this.

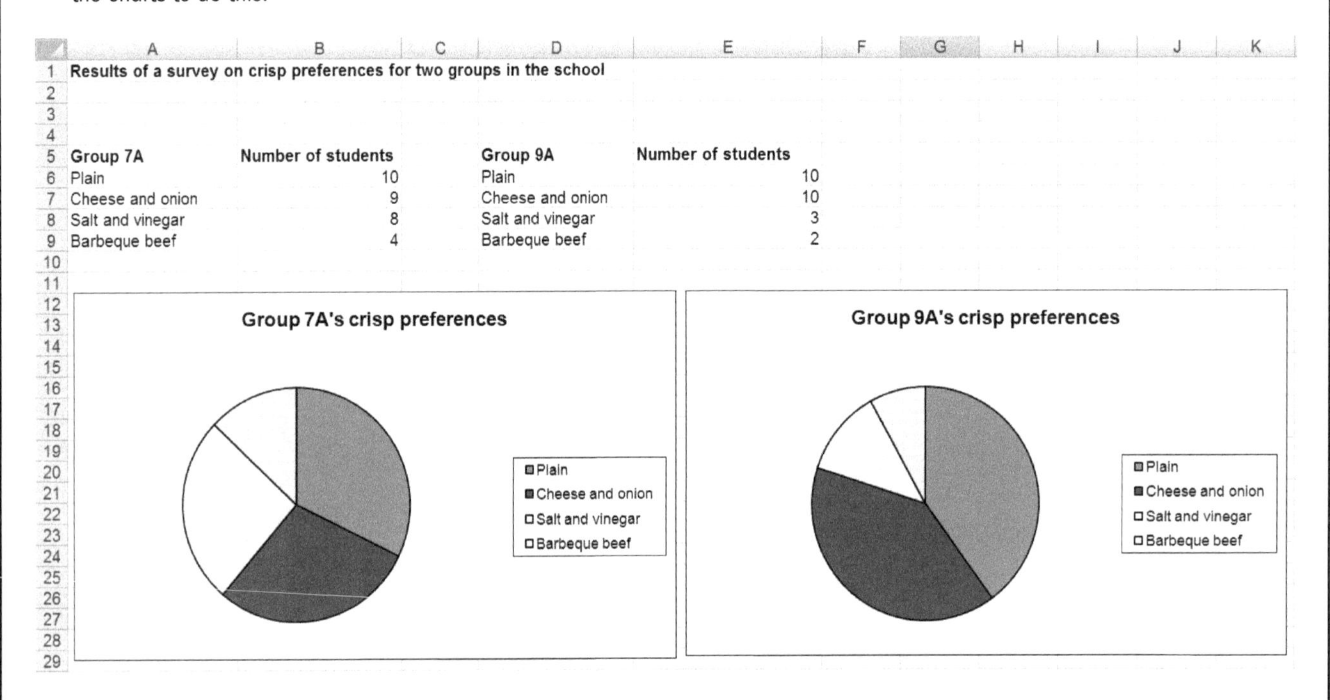

Save your file using the filename **'Pie chart showing the results of the crisp survey'**.

Document production

This worksheet can be best used following study of formatting text and organising page layout on pages 168 to 173 of Chapter 17 in the Student Book.

Worksheet 17.1

Document production

There are a number of terms that you need to understand when producing documents in the examination.

Here are some terms. Your task is to fill in the worksheet by writing their meanings next to each term.

Term	Meaning
Page orientation	
Gutter margin	
Sans serif	
Serif	
Cell alignment	

Worksheet 17.1 answers

Teacher resource pack page 103

Term	Meaning
Page orientation	The way a page is printed onto paper. Either landscape where the width is larger than the height, or portrait where the height is larger than the width.
Gutter margin	More space added in addition to the margin so that when a document is bound all of the content on the page can be seen.
Sans serif	Fonts which do not use the small lines at the end of characters.
Serif	A small decorative line added to the basic form of a character in a font.
Cell alignment	Determines the position of text in a cell in a table.

Databases

Topic 18 answers

Questions A

Student book page 182

1 One mark for each correct answer.

Name of field	Example data	Data type
Title	(Mr, Mrs, Ms, Dr, etc.)	Alphanumeric/text
Phone number	0798273232	Alphanumeric/text
Sex	M or F	Logical/Boolean
Country	Botswana	Alphanumeric/text
Date of birth	01/10/03	Date
Years at address	4	Numeric

2 One mark for each correct answer.

Items of data	Tick if data type is logical/Boolean
Driving licence (yes or no)	√
Sex (M or F)	√
Size (S, M, L, XL, XXL)	
Airport code	
Car registration number	
Date of purchase	
Car type (manual or automatic)	√
Fuel type (diesel or petrol)	√

Questions B

Student book page 185

1 **a** One mark each for two from: Reg-number, Make, Model or Year

b One mark for Reg-number

c One mark for an explanation such as:

It is the only field which is unique.

No two registration numbers are the same.

d One mark for 7

2 **a** One mark for a total of three correct fields:

i Alphanumeric

ii Alphanumeric

iii Boolean/Logical

b Three fields (one mark each) such as:

Form teacher

Form

Date of entry into school

Exam results

Number of half days in school

Pupil email address

Pupil mobile number

Name of parent/guardian

Parent/guardian work telephone number

Medical problems

Medication taken

c One mark for the name of the field and one mark for an explanation.

UniquePupilNumber – no two pupils can have the same number, so it is used to identify pupils who could have the same names.

d One mark each for two errors such as:

Transcription errors – where data copied from forms is misread

Transposition errors – where digits are incorrectly reversed when being typed into the database

e One mark for each method that is applicable to the answer in part (d).

Verification where, after the data is keyed in, it is carefully checked against the original document used to supply the information, such as an application form

Validation checks, such as a check digit added to the unique pupil number which checks that all the other numbers in the pupil number have been inputted correctly

3 **a** One mark for one of the following:

A database consisting of a single table of data

A list of data created using spreadsheet software

b One mark for:

A database where the data is held in two or more tables with relationships forming links between the tables.

c One mark for a statement of the application and one mark for a reason why the application is suitable. An example answer is as follows:

For a simple list of contact details (1), so that they can be searched easily and used as the contact details for a mail merge (1)

4 **a** One mark for each difference to a maximum of two marks.

Flat file has all the data in a single table (1) whereas a relational database contains the data in two or more tables (1).

There are no relationships in a flat file database because there is only one table (1) whereas in a relational database there are relationships between the tables (1).

b One mark for each of three points similar to the following:

Relational database (1)

Three tables are needed: Customer, dresses and rentals (1)

Would avoid duplicated data/redundancy (1)

Less data would need to be input (1)

It would be easier to keep the data up-to-date (1)

The data could be extracted more flexibly (1)

Presentations

This worksheet can be best used following study of presentations in Chapter 19 in the Student Book.

Worksheet 19.1

How much do you know about the presentation software PowerPoint?

You will be using the presentation software PowerPoint in your course. You probably know quite a lot about the software already. See how much basic knowledge you have by answering the following questions on this worksheet.

What does each of the following do?

1. Arial ____________________
2. ____________________
3. A ____________________
4. Design ____________________
5. Table ____________________
6. A Text Box ____________________
7. Slide Sorter ____________________
8. ____________________
9. A ____________________
10. ____________________

Topic 19 answers

Worksheet 19.1: How much do you know about the presentation software PowerPoint?

Teacher resource pack page 107

	Icon	Answer
1	Arial	Change the font type
2		Centre text
3	A^	Increase the font size
4	Design	Slide design (pick a template, colour scheme or animation)
5	Table	Create tables or borders
6	A Text Box	Create a text box
7	Slide Sorter	Slide sorter view
8		Slide show starting from the current slide
9	A	Font colour
10		Bullet points

Spreadsheets

This worksheet can be best used following study of spreadsheets in Chapter 20 in the Student Book.

Worksheet 20.1

Spreadsheets

1 Explain the difference between an absolute cell reference and a relative cell reference.

____

____

____

____

2 The following spreadsheet was set up to work out in which subject boys or girls did best. The spreadsheet also shows the average percentage achieved by girls and boys in all the subjects.

	A	B	C
1	**Advanced Level exam results 2021**		
2	Percentage pass rate with "A" grades		
3			
4	**Subject**	**Boys**	**Girls**
5	Art and design	23.5	28.4
6	Biology	16.8	20.0
7	Busines studies	10.0	11.3
8	Chemistry	25.6	27.7
9	Computing	8.9	7.5
10	Econonics	22.7	22.6
11	English	17.3	16.2
12	French	26.4	23.9
13	Geography	15.8	23.0
14	German	32.9	26.8
15	History	17.9	19.1
16	Mathematics	28.9	30.0
17	Physics	24.1	27.4
18	Psychology	8.1	13.7
19	**Average percentage**	15.8	21.3

a Give the function that was entered into cell B19 to work out the average percentage for boys.

____

b The following formula was entered into cell D5. Explain what this formula does.

=IF(B5>C5,"Boys","Girls")

Explanation: ____

____

____

____

Worksheet 20.1 (continued)

3 You can specify that cells can only contain a certain type of data.

Fill in the following table to show an example of the type of data that could be entered.

Type of data	Example of data
Date	
Integer number (a whole number)	
Decimal number	
Percentage	
Currency	
Text	

4 Write down the answers each of the following formulae would give when entered into a spreadsheet cell:

a =5%*200

____

b =B4+F6*5 where cell B4 = 10 and cell F6 = 20

____

c =C3*C4+12 where cell C3 = 8 and cell C4 = 7

____

5 Here are some statements concerning the reasons for putting formulae into spreadsheets.

Put a tick next to those reasons that are correct.

Reason	Tick if reason is correct
If a cell changes, then all those cells that depend on the cell will change.	
A more accurate answer is produced than with a calculator.	
It improves the appearance of the spreadsheet.	
The formulae in the spreadsheet need to be kept secret.	

6 In some spreadsheets a cell or a range of cells is given a name rather than a cell reference such as B4. Give one advantage of this.

____

____

____

7 Explain what is meant by a cell label.

____

____

Worksheet 20.1 answers

Teacher resource pack page 109

1 An absolute reference always refers to a particular cell. It therefore always refers to the same cell even when the formula containing the cell is copied to a new location.

A relative reference refers to a cell that is a certain number of rows and columns away.

2 **a** =AVERAGE(B5:B18)

b If the number in cell B5 (i.e. the boys' mark) is greater than the number in cell C5 (i.e. the girls' mark), then the text 'Boys' will be placed in cell D5. If not, the text 'Girls' will be displayed in cell D5.

3 Any examples of the correct data type. Such as:

Type of data	Example of data
Date	30/12/16
Integer number (a whole number)	34
Decimal number	3.14
Percentage	4%
Currency	$3.45
Text	John Smith

4 **a** 10

b 110

c 68

5

Reason	Tick if reason is correct
If a cell changes, then all those cells that depend on the cell will change.	√
A more accurate answer is produced than with a calculator.	
It improves the appearance of the spreadsheet.	
The formulae in the spreadsheet need to be kept secret.	

6 If cells are given names then when you look at a formula, the formula becomes easier to understand.

7 A cell label is a cell next to a cell containing data to say what the data in the cell represents.

21 Website authoring

This worksheet can be best used following study of website authoring in Chapter 21 in the Student Book.

Worksheet 21.1

HTML

1 **a** What does the abbreviation HTML stand for?

____

b HTML uses things called tags. What is the purpose of these tags?

____

____

c Websites make use of hyperlinks. What are hyperlinks and how do they make using websites easier?

____

____

____

d A web page needs to contain a link to the following website: www.bbc.co.uk

Write down the HTML to produce this link.

____

2 Stylesheets are often used when creating websites.

a Explain what is meant by a stylesheet.

____

____

____

b Describe two advantages in using stylesheets.

Advantage 1: ____

____

____

Worksheet 21.1 (continued)

Advantage 2: ______________________________

____

____

3 Give the meaning of each of the following tags used with HTML when creating websites.

a <b> and </b> ______________________________

b <u> and </u> ______________________________

c <i> and </i> ______________________________

d
 ____

e <hr> ______________________________

Worksheet 21.1 answers

Teacher resource pack page 112

1 **a** Hypertext Markup Language

b Tags are instructions that tell the computer how it wants text and images in an HTML document formatted or positioned.

c Hyperlinks are links from one place in one document to a different place in the same document or a completely different document. If you click on a hyperlink, it takes you to a different place.

d <a href =http://www.bbc.co.uk >Click here</a>

2 **a** A document which sets out fonts and font sizes for headings, subheadings, main body text, etc. in a document

b They save time – you only have to change things in one document (i.e. the stylesheet).

They help give a website a consistent look (e.g. heading sizes, fonts, font sizes, etc. will be consistent across all pages).

3 **a** <b> and </b> means start bold and stop bold style text.

b <u> and </u> means start underline and stop underline style text.

c <i> and </i> means start italics and stop italics style text.

d
 means insert a line break. There is no closing tag for this. This creates a smaller gap than the <p> tag.

e <hr> means insert a horizontal line and there is no closing tag.

Case studies

Although case studies do not feature in the examinations, they can be used with your students to add breadth and interest to their studies. The case studies included here can help your students consolidate their learning.

Case study 1

Identity fraud

At a recent trial five people who had stolen the identities of the living and the dead were found guilty of fraud and were sentenced to between 4 and 8 years in prison.

The gang forged driving licences, pay slips and utility bills (e.g. gas and electricity bills) to steal the real identities of people who lived at properties which were now vacant.

The gang stole the identities of 60 people around the country and used them to take out bank loans, overdrafts and credit cards.

The money they made was huge and the ringleader drove a $250,000 sports car and wore a $45,000 watch.

The judge when passing sentence said that the crimes were complex and sophisticated.

Questions

1 Identity theft has risen by a large amount over recent years.
Give two pieces of advice to a person who does not want to be a victim of identity theft/fraud. *(2 marks)*

2 Once a person's identity has been stolen, the thief can do several things with the new identity. Describe one thing that the thief can do that will affect the victim. *(2 marks)*

Case study 2

Illegal downloads

The music industry has been hit hard by internet file sharing and illegal downloads.

For example, some young people use free, but illegal, online converters to convert videos of songs from YouTube to an mp3 format. They then share this music with their friends. This deprives the music industry of a large amount of money and prevents them investing in new artists.

The music industry has tended to focus its attention on the file- [i.e. file-sharing] sharing sites which allow people to illegally copy music or video files from each other. Such sites allow users to use peer-to-peer networking to transfer files.

According to a 2019 worldwide study, 23% of 16 to 64 year olds obtained their music by stream-ripping. Stream-ripping is illegal and involves creating a file from online content which can then be downloaded. This practice leads to a massive amount of money being lost by the music industry.

An organisation called the BMR (British Music Rights) helps the music industry take the owners of file-sharing sites to court but it is worried that individuals who know that file copying is illegal still do it.

The worry is that professional musicians and songwriters will reach the point where they cannot make a living and they will have to give up. This will be to the detriment of everyone who enjoys listening to music.

Questions

1 Music can be downloaded legally or illegally.

- **a** Explain what the term 'downloading' means. *(2 marks)*
- **b** Describe one situation where music can be downloaded legally and one situation where music can be downloaded illegally. *(2 marks)*

2 Anyone who is involved in the music industry is affected by illegal downloads.

- **a** Explain one way in which a recording company would be affected by these illegal downloads. *(1 mark)*
- **b** Explain one way in which a musician, group or singer would be affected by these illegal downloads. *(1 mark)*

3 In the UK, The Copyright Designs and Patents Act makes it an offence to illegally download or copy music. It forbids the copying of other things as well. Give the names of two different things which are copied illegally. *(2 marks)*

Case study 3

How using social networking sites might cause you health problems

You already know that using computers can cause a number of health problems such as backache, repetitive strain injury (RSI) and eye strain. Some doctors think that the use of social networking sites could cause serious health problems.

Increased isolation from people could raise your risk of serious health problems because of lack of face-to-face contact. It may impair immune responses and alter hormones.

Social networking sites allow people to keep in touch with friends over the internet. But although they are supposed to bring people together, they may be doing the reverse. The hours spent communicating with 'virtual' friends is reducing the amount of time spent with real people.

More people are also teleworking (working remotely or from home), which means that most of their communication with other workers is via email, VoIP and video-conferencing.

One doctor has stated that, 'Levels of hormones such as the "cuddle chemical" oxytocin, which promotes bonding, altered according to whether people were in close contact or not'. He went on to say that, 'There does seem to be a difference between "real presence" and the virtual variety'.

Questions

1 One health problem caused by the use of computers is RSI.
Give the meaning of the term RSI. *(1 mark)*

2 Explain two things you can do using a social networking site. *(2 marks)*

3 Many teleworkers use ICT systems, which means they do not have to meet face-to-face (i.e. in person).

- **a** Explain what is meant by teleworking. *(2 marks)*
- **b** Many teleworkers make use of VoIP. Give the meaning of the abbreviation VoIP. *(1 mark)*
- **c** Explain one reason why many teleworkers choose to use VoIP. *(1 mark)*
- **d** Teleworkers often make use of a system which allows them to conduct 'virtual' face-to-face meetings. Give the name of this system and explain how it benefits teleworkers. *(3 marks)*

4 Explain why some doctors believe that lack of social contact with real people might cause some health problems. *(2 marks)*

Case study 4

Cyber warfare

Most developed countries are totally dependent on their ICT systems, and the loss of such systems could do serious damage to the infrastructure of countries.

For example, could you imagine the loss of the internet for a lengthy period or the loss of the entire mobile phone network? What about the erasure of all the health information on health service computers? Or the erasure of tax information so that the government could not collect money to pay for schools, hospitals, the police, etc.?

In many ways, attacks on ICT systems could do a lot more damage than a series of terrorist bombs or even a war using conventional weapons.

Many terrorist groups use the internet for recruitment, propaganda and communication purposes. They may also conduct cyber-attacks against their enemies.

Some countries have started to investigate the use of the internet to cause damage to the infrastructure of other countries. Targets would typically involve key businesses, the national power grid (for electricity supply), financial markets and government departments. The UK government has decided to set up a new office for cyber security. This department will monitor, analyse and counter any cyber-attacks.

It is interesting to note that as well as protecting against cyber warfare, many countries are investigating the potential of using cyber warfare itself, should the need arise.

Many governments have turned to hackers who have the experience to know how to get past security methods and break into networks.

Cyber-attacks have already occurred. For example, the European Banking Authority's email servers were compromised in a global Microsoft Exchange cyber-attack early in 2021.

Questions

1 **a** Explain what hacking is and why it is so important to keep hackers out of key networks. *(3 marks)*

b Networks can be protected using firewalls.
Explain how a firewall can be used to prevent unauthorised access. *(2 marks)*

2 Give two examples of systems that could be hacked into and deliberately damaged as part of a cyber-attack. *(2 marks)*

3 Some people think it is morally wrong to give good well-paid jobs to hackers who have deliberately broken the law.
Say with reasons whether you agree or disagree with this. *(2 marks)*

4 Terrorists use encryption to ensure the privacy of communication and to prevent being detected and caught.

a Explain what encryption is and how it ensures the privacy of communication. *(2 marks)*

b Some countries are worried that encryption of data causes as many problems as it solves. Explain why a country might ban encryption. *(2 marks)*

Case study 5

Wikipedia

Wikipedia was set up to empower and engage people around the world by collecting and offering free content which can be disseminated globally. It is a huge success story and has changed the way the internet is used.

You will probably have already used Wikipedia but if not, take a look at its website now.

Wikipedia is a charity, and, unlike most other free providers of content, it does not contain adverts and therefore gets no money from these sources. Instead it relies mainly on asking you and me to donate money or on revenue from grants. The money it obtains is used to buy hardware and also for hosting the website and bandwidth costs. People are not paid to add content – they do it for free!

Wikipedia is best described as an online encyclopaedia, but it is different to other encyclopaedias in so much as it is made up of contributions by ordinary people.

You may think this is a bad thing. After all, what if the information is wrong? It is easy to put in bogus information or information which someone believes is true but isn't. Luckily, other people can add information which corrects the information that is already there.

The idea is that if enough people contribute, then the information is as good as that provided more traditionally.

Questions

1 Wikipedia is a good example of lots of people working collaboratively using ICT.

a Explain what 'collaboratively' means. *(1 mark)*

b Give one reason why some people like to contribute towards Wikipedia. *(1 mark)*

2 One commenter on Wikipedia said:, There is plenty of bogus information on the internet. What we don't want is non-experts making any old rubbish up on Wikipedia and then our children getting hold of it and believing it to be true.'
Give a reason why this is less likely to happen than the commenter thinks. *(2 marks)*

3 You have been asked to give a brief description of what Wikipedia is to someone who has little knowledge of ICT.
Describe Wikipedia in easy-to-understand, non-technical language.
You should make at least three main points in your description. *(3 marks)*

Case study 6

Phishing – tricking people to part with account information

Phishing is where fraudsters set up a fake website which looks the same as a bank website and then send out lots of emails to attract people to the site. When they go onto the fake site, they are asked to supply personal/financial details which can be used to steal their identity and money.

The name phishing arises because they are 'fishing' for personal information.

Shown below is an example of a 'phishing' email.

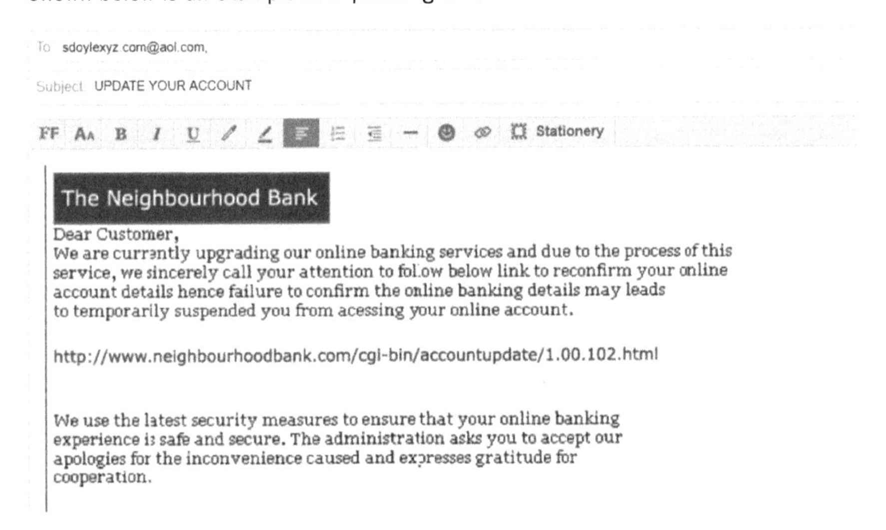

To sdoylexyz com@aol.com,

Subject UPDATE YOUR ACCOUNT

FF AA B I U Stationery

The Neighbourhood Bank

Dear Customer,
We are currently upgrading our online banking services and due to the process of this service, we sincerely call your attention to follow below link to reconfirm your online account details hence failure to confirm the online banking details may leads to temporarily suspended you from acessing your online account.

http://www.neighbourhoodbank.com/cgi-bin/accountupdate/1.00.102.html

We use the latest security measures to ensure that your online banking experience is safe and secure. The administration asks you to accept our apologies for the inconvenience caused and expresses gratitude for cooperation.

The phishing email looks genuine, but read it and see if there is anything that would make you suspicious?

When you click on the link in the email, you are directed to the following website:

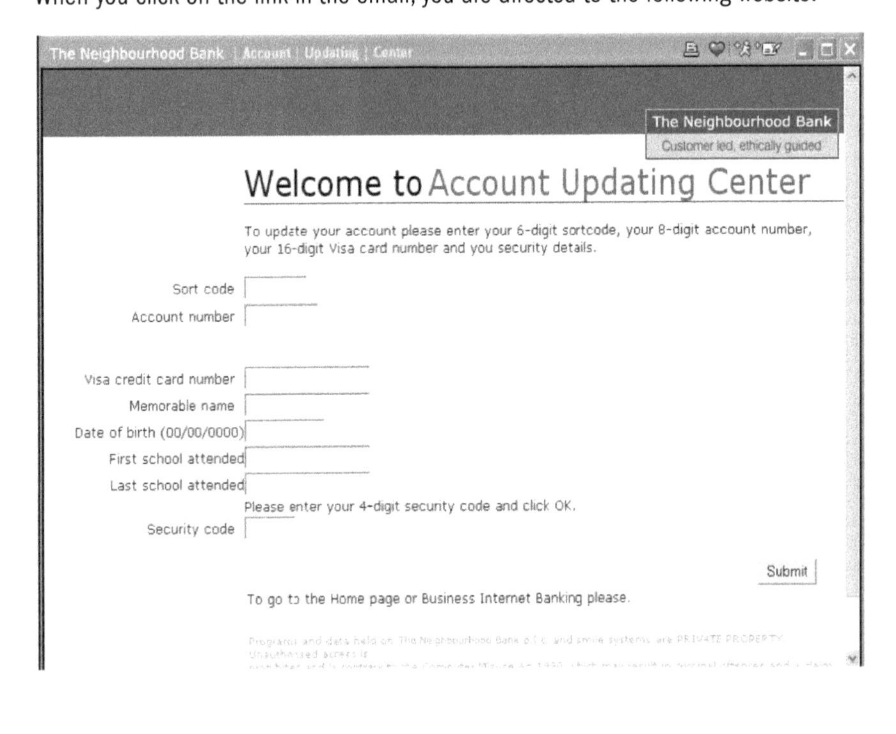

Case study 6 (continued)

If you were to supply this personal information, the fraudster would have enough detail to be able to steal your identity and buy goods and services using your credit card.

Note that there is no indication that encryption is going to be used to scramble the information entered.

To combat phishing, banks now address you by name when sending you an email and also write down the last few numbers of your account number. Anyone sending you these fake emails would be unlikely to have these details normally, so you can be sure you are looking at an email from your bank.

Questions

1 As more people use the internet for banking and buying goods and services online, there has been a huge increase in phishing.
Describe the meaning of the term phishing and give an example of how it works. *(2 marks)*

2 When credit card or other personal/financial details are sent over the internet, they are always encrypted before sending.

a Explain what is meant by the term encryption. *(2 marks)*

b Give one reason why encryption is necessary. *(2 marks)*

c Many banks ask a security question before a transaction can be completed. Give an example of a security question. *(1 mark)*

3 Banks and credit card companies are very worried about phishing.
Give two pieces of advice you would give to people who buy goods/services or who bank online, to help prevent them falling for these fake emails and sites. *(2 marks)*

Case study 7

Using fingerprinting in schools

Many schools are now using fingerprinting methods to help with pupil registration.

The system works by the pupils placing their finger on a scanner which is installed outside the classrooms. The scanner reads certain aspects of the print to identify the pupil and then records the attendance details on the computer.

The head teacher of the school has sung the praises of the system, saying how it has helped reduce truancy because pupils now know that it can be immediately identified by the system. Teachers at the school have welcomed the system because it frees them from having to do this important but time-consuming task.

If a pupil fails to register at the start of the day, a text message can be sent to the parent's mobile phone, alerting them of the non-attendance of their child. This makes it virtually impossible for a pupil not to attend school without their parents knowing.

Many pupils like the system because it gives them more time in the morning to chat with friends and find out what is going on in the school from their form teacher.

Some parents and pupils were initially worried that fingerprints were being routinely taken and stored by the school and that this was personal data which could be misused.

However, the company who supplied the system explained to parents that no full fingerprints are stored by the system. Instead the fingerprint is stored as a code and it is this code that is matched. They were reassured that a fingerprint cannot be re-created from this code and that it is only used by the school for identification purposes and not for some other sinister use.

Questions

1 Many schools use fingerprinting as a method for recording the presence of pupils at school.

- **a** Fingerprinting is an example of a biometric input device.
  Explain briefly what this sentence means. *(2 marks)*
- **b** Give three advantages of using fingerprinting for registering attendance in schools. *(3 marks)*
- **c** Many parents may be worried that the system stores their child's fingerprints. Write a sentence to explain how you might address this worry. *(2 marks)*

2 Describe one way in which the fingerprinting system helps prevent truancy in schools. *(2 marks)*

3 Give one example of how this fingerprinting attendance system could possibly be misused. *(2 marks)*

Case study 8

A fashion magazine making the most of communication

Bling, a new fashion magazine, brings the latest in fashion to its readers. There are two sides to the business: the editorial side and the business side.

The editorial side is where the freelance writers and journalists supply text for inclusion in the magazine, and the freelance photographers and graphic designers produce the photographs and artwork.

The business side is where the sales staff visit the newsagents and other retailers to take orders for the magazine. There are also other sales staff who sell advertising space in the magazine. There are also staff who deal with invoices and accounts and these are based at the head office in London.

The following communication services are used in the business:

- SMS/texting – staff spend time with customers or in meetings and do not want to take phone calls during this time, so texting is a good way of contacting them.
- File sharing – the editorial staff work with freelancers on the magazine. They use file-sharing websites to send large files of images such as high-resolution photographs that would be too big to attach to an email.
- VoIP – phone calls are often made to other countries, and the use of VoIP has reduced the costs of these calls, along with calls made locally.
- Video-conferencing – meetings between the freelance staff and the staff employed at head office are difficult as the freelance staff live all over the country and a few of them live abroad. Traditional meetings take up too much time and mean people have to spend time away from their families. Video-conferencing enables staff to do all the things they do at meetings electronically.
- Email – this communication is used the most. Communication can be short and to the point. The freelance staff can attach files to the email. These attached files can contain text, photographs, graphics, etc.
- All people who work for the magazine can access the company network. This can be done remotely (i.e. away from the head office) using the internet. In order to access the network, they need to enter their user-ID and a password. This allows sales staff to enter the orders placed by newsagents directly from their laptops, tablets and phones. The advantage in doing this is that it avoids paperwork, and fewer mistakes are made.
- All PCs and laptops, tablets and phones have the following software installed to aid communication:
  - Web browser software – so that searches of the internet can be made for ideas for designs, looking at competitor magazines, looking at high street fashions, etc.
  - Email software – so that a user can send and receive email, attach files, send emails to groups of co-workers, etc.
  - Messaging software – so that VoIP phone calls can be made using the internet, so that texts can be sent and received and so that instant messaging can be used.

Questions

1 **a** Give the name of the software used to view web pages. *(1 mark)*

b Give the name of the service which is most often used for sending and receiving digital messages from one computer to another using the internet. *(1 mark)*

2 When changing a password, explain why the user has to enter the password twice. *(2 marks)*

3 Describe three advantages in using emails rather than telephone calls in order to give some important information. *(3 marks)*

Case study 8 (continued)

4 Explain the difference between a text message and an IM (Instant Message). *(2 marks)*

5 Video-conferencing is used by many organisations to conduct face-to-face meetings at a distance.

a Explain two advantages of video-conferencing. *(2 marks)*

b Explain two disadvantages of video-conferencing. *(2 marks)*

6 When people are working remotely using ICT it can expose data to certain risks.

a Give two methods by which you can ensure the security of the data held on the network. *(2 marks)*

b There is a danger that when data is transferred using the internet, it may be intercepted. Data is often encrypted when sent.
Explain what encryption means and why it helps secure data. *(2 marks)*

Case study answers

Case study 1: Identity fraud

1 One mark for each of two pieces of advice such as:

Do not respond to emails asking for banking details/credit card details/passwords, etc.

Always check that a banking or other site has the correct URL before using it.

Use security/virus-checking software to ensure that software which records your passwords is not present.

Check a site uses encryption before entering credit card/banking details.

Shred any paperwork before putting it in the rubbish.

2 One mark for the thing they can do and one mark for the consequences.

For example:

The thief can use the details online (1) for the purchase of goods or services (1).

They can steal the victim's identity (1) and open fraudulent accounts and loans (1).

Case study 2: Illegal downloads

1 a One mark for each point to a maximum of two marks.

Taking a file from a larger computer

And transferring it over a network to your smaller computer

b One mark for a legal download such as:

Bought on a site on the internet

Obtained from a site where the music has been donated freely by the artist

One mark for an illegal download such as:

An illegal file-sharing site

2 a One mark for: They would lose money they would have obtained from the legal sales.

b One mark for: They would not get any money/royalties for the illegal downloads.

3 One mark each for two things which are copied illegally such as:

Large section of text

Photographs

Software

Human computer interfaces

Films/video

Case study 3: How using social networking sites might cause you health problems

1 One mark for: Repetitive strain injury

2 One mark for each item to a maximum of two marks such as:

Meet new friends

Look at the profiles of other people

Search for people with similar interests to yourself

Look at other people's photographs

Send each other messages

Create a profile for yourself

etc.

3 a Two marks for an answer similar to the following:

Working from home (1) by making use of ICT facilities and services (1)

b One mark for: Voice over Internet Protocol

c One mark for: Phone calls are much cheaper

d One mark for each point to a maximum of three marks.

Teleconferencing/video-conferencing

No time spent travelling to meetings

No costs such as travelling costs or hotel costs

No time spent away from home

Can work collaboratively without needing to be in the same place

4 One mark for each point to a maximum of two marks.

There are chemicals which fight disease (1) which are released when humans are in contact with each other (1).

These are not released during virtual meetings (1).

Case study 4: Cyber warfare

1 a One mark for each point to a maximum of three marks.

Unauthorised access to an ICT system

Usually but not necessarily using the internet

Hackers can delete important data

This data can relate to terrorists, organised crime, etc.

It could be medical details for the whole country

This can easily cause loss of life

It could cause loss of infrastructure such as loss of air traffic control

b One mark for each point to a maximum of three marks.

Firewall is hardware, software or both

Used to prevent unauthorised access to a network

Blocks requests for certain data

Examines each incoming package of data

If package is not of a type allowed, it is rejected

2 One mark for each of two examples such as:

Nuclear power stations

MI5

Central medical databases

The Pentagon

Armed forces computer systems

NASA

etc.

3 One mark for each point to a maximum of two marks.

Agree:

Hackers have a good understanding of methods used.

They can point out vulnerabilities.

They know other hackers and can 'grass' on them.

Disagree

Rewarding them is morally wrong.

It encourages hackers as they know they will get a well-paid job.

Hacking could become a career pathway.

You cannot pay criminals.

4 a One mark for each point to a maximum of two marks.

Encryption scrambles the data into a code.

You need a key to turn the data back to readable form.

If a hacker intercepted the data, they would not be able to understand it.

If the data was stolen (e.g. on a laptop) the data would be unreadable.

Useful for sending banking details over the internet

b One mark for each point to a maximum of two marks.

Encryption can be used by terrorists or criminals.

It enables them to have conversations in private.

Prevents surveillance from taking place

Makes it harder for security services to collect evidence

Harder to gain prosecutions

Case study 5: Wikipedia

1 a One mark for one of the following:

Actively working together

More than one person working on the same project

b One mark for one of the following:

They find it interesting.

It is a hobby.

They like to help everyone using their specialist knowledge.

They like to build up their knowledge of a subject.

2 One mark each for two relevant points such as:

Others can add information which corrects what has been added.

There are lots of viewers so mistakes are quickly spotted.

3 One mark for each point to a maximum of three:

It is an online encyclopaedia

Created collaboratively/by lots of people

Uses money from donations to keep it running

People add their own content

Others can make corrections

etc.

Case study 6: Phishing – tricking people to part with account information

1 One mark for definition and one mark for suitable example.

Phishing means sending fake emails to lots of different people in the hope that some of them might divulge credit card details and passwords. These details could then be used to commit a range of frauds such as buying goods or services using the details or even taking out loans by forging a person's identity.

2 a One mark for mentioning 'coding' and other mark for 'unable to read encrypted data' or similar.

Encryption means coding data so that even if it were intercepted, the person would be unable to read or understand the encrypted data.

b Two marks for answer similar to the following:

To ensure the privacy and the security of credit card and bank account details when ordering goods or services over the internet or performing online banking.

c One mark for any security question such as:

Mother's maiden name

Name of first school attended, etc.

3 Two marks for any advice similar to two of the following:

Never give details of account numbers, credit card numbers, expiry dates, etc. to anyone.

Watch out for fake emails with spelling mistakes, grammatical errors, etc.

Be very careful when entering passwords, etc. into sites as they may not be genuine sites.

Case study 7: Using fingerprinting in schools

1 **a** Any two points (one mark each) similar to:

Uses properties of the human body (1) which are unique for a particular person (1) such as fingerprints or pattern on retina (1) to uniquely identify that person (1)

b Any three from the following list (one mark each):

Scanning and recognition are performed quickly

Pupils cannot register for others

Because the system is so quick it means pupils can be registered for each lesson

Improves attendance rates as system automatically sends texts about non-attendance to parents

Frees teachers from taking registers

Give pupils more responsibility for their attendance

c Two marks for two points similar to the following:

Fingerprint images are not stored.

Only certain points of the image are stored.

The pattern of the points is coded and stored.

Manufacturers say that fingerprints cannot be re-created from the stored code.

2 One mark for each point to a max of two marks for:

System records pupil attendance in almost real time (1). Parents can be immediately informed if their child is not in school (1) using a text message which the system sends automatically (1) - acts as a deterrent against truancy (1).

3 Two marks for two valid points:

All children could be routinely scanned for fingerprints (1), meaning the government could eventually have a database of everyone's fingerprints (1), which would erode privacy (1) but could be used by the police to solve crimes (1).

Case study 8: A fashion magazine making the most of communication

1 **a** One mark for web browser software

b One mark for email software

2 One mark for each point to a maximum of two marks.

To ensure they have typed in the password they meant to type in (1) as they are unlikely to make the same mistake twice (1)

As a method of verification (1) to ensure that the correct password has been typed (1)

3 One mark for each of three advantages such as:

They can be printed out.

They can be forwarded easily to others.

They are received almost instantly.

They can be saved for future reference.

People can receive them from lots of different devices (mobile phones, tablets, etc.).

4 One mark for an incomplete explanation of the difference and two marks for a more complete explanation.

Text messages are sent using a service called SMS.

IMs are sent using the internet.

You can have conversations in real time using IMs.

5 **a** One mark for each of two advantages such as:

No time is wasted travelling to meetings.

It is greener because fewer journeys are made.

Meetings can be organised and held at the last minute.

People do not have to spend time away from their families.

b One mark for each of two disadvantages such as:

Some people like to travel to meetings.

You cannot handle a real product virtually.

The social interaction with real people is important to people who work remotely.

6 **a** One mark each for two methods such as:

Ensure regular backups are kept.

Ensure a firewall is installed to protect against hackers.

Install the latest virus-scanning software and keep it up-to-date.

Ensure the computer is protected by passwords.

Encrypt any personal data stored.

b One mark each for two points made similar to the following:

It scrambles the data before being transferred

So that if it is intercepted, the data cannot be understood

Exam support

Here are some examination-style questions along with sample answers and teacher commentary on those answers. Each example is followed by some suggested answers.

Topic 1

Types and components of computer systems

WORKED EXAMPLE

Graphical user interfaces (GUIs) are a feature of the operating system on most computers.

a Explain why a computer needs a user interface. *(2 marks)*

b Give **one** input device, other than a keyboard, that can be used with a graphical user interface. *(1 mark)*

c Give **four** features of a graphical user interface. *(4 marks)*

d **i** Give **one** other type of user interface. *(1 mark)*

ii Give **two** benefits to an inexperienced user offered by a graphical user interface compared with this type of interface. *(2 marks)*

Sample answer 1

a The user interface provides an interface between the computer and the user.

It allows the user to use the computer.

b Mouse

c Pull-down menus

Windows

Icons

Menus

d **i** Menu-driven interface

ii Menus only allow a few things to be done whereas with a GUI you can have lots of icons to click on.

Teacher comment

a This simply repeats the words from the question, but does not answer it! I cannot give any marks for this.

b This is a correct piece of hardware so one mark is awarded.

c Pull-down menus and menus are not distinctly different so only one mark can be given rather than two. The other answers are correct. Three marks are given.

d **i** This is a correct type of interface so one mark is given.

ii This is only one benefit so only one mark is awarded. You must always check that they have given the correct number of answers.

(6 marks out of 10)

Sample answer 2

a The user interface is the point where the user and the computer meet. The user interface provides a way of the user interacting with the computer. For example, they can issue commands by clicking on menu items and icons.

b Touch screen

c Windows

Icons

Pointers

Menus

d **i** Windows

ii The icons in a GUI have small pictures that help a user understand what they do. Graphical user interfaces are almost the norm so once a user has learnt one type of interface they will be able to use others easily.

Teacher comment

a There are three valid points made so the maximum of two marks is given here.

b A touch screen can be considered to be an input device (and also an output device) and they have become increasingly popular, so this is a valid answer and one mark is awarded.

c Four correct features of a GUI have been given, so four marks are awarded.

d **i** Never give a brand name unless the question specifically asks for it. This means that Windows is not an acceptable answer so no marks for this answer.

ii There are two points made here and the argument about the GUI in the last point could be put forward about a menu-driven interface. I would give this answer both marks.

(9 marks out of 10)

Answers

a One mark for each of the following points to a maximum of two marks:

- Allows a user to communicate with the computer
- The way the computer interacts with the user
- It allows the user to make selections
- It provides a dialogue between the computer and the user

b One mark for one of the following:

- Mouse
- Keyboard
- Light pen
- Touch screen
- etc.

c Any four from the following (one mark each):

- Windows
- Icons
- Menus/Pull-down menus
- Pointers
- Online help/Office assistants

d **i** One mark for one of the following:

- Menu-driven interface
- Command line interface
- Voice driven interface/interface making use of voice recognition

ii One mark each for two benefits such as:

- Standard look and feel
- Interfaces are similar so they are easier to learn and skills can be transferred
- More intuitive (users can usually figure out what they have to do)
- Use of icons with pictures makes it easy for users to work out what each button does

Topic 2

Input and output devices

WORKED EXAMPLE

Webcams can take live video which can be transferred using the internet to a computer in the home.

a Tick the **three** applications that are possible using a webcam. *(3 marks)*

	Tick **three** boxes
Watching the evolution of dinosaurs	
A parent checking up on their children in a nursery when they are at work	
Looking at live video of an erupting volcano in a geography lesson	
Watching a movie star constantly wherever they go	
Watching the space shuttle taking off as it happens	

b Give **two** advantages of using a webcam. *(2 marks)*

c Give **two** disadvantages of using a webcam. *(2 marks)*

Sample answer 1

a

	Tick **three** boxes
Watching the evolution of dinosaurs	√
A parent checking up on their children in a nursery when they are at work	
Looking at live video of an erupting volcano in a geography lesson	
Watching a movie star constantly wherever they go	√
Watching the space shuttle taking off as it happens	√

b You can use it to spy on other people.

They are very cheap to buy and many computers have them built into the screen.

c They do not produce a very good image.

You cannot store the image produced.

Teacher comment

a Webcams produce live images, so you obviously cannot watch the evolution of dinosaurs.

Watching a movie star wherever they go would require a webcam to be present all the time. Clearly this is false.

The last tick is in the correct box.

b The first answer is a bit vague and needed further amplification to get the mark. The second answer is OK and gains a mark.

c The first answer is correct and gains a mark.

It is possible to save an image produced by a webcam and this is how they are used for security purposes.

(3 marks out of 7)

Sample answer 2

a

	Tick **three** boxes
Watching the evolution of dinosaurs	
A parent checking up on their children in a nursery when they are at work	√
Looking at live video of an erupting volcano in a geography lesson	√
Watching a movie star constantly wherever they go	
Watching the space shuttle taking off as it happens	√

b You can look at famous sites throughout the world using live or almost live pictures.

They can be used for surveillance by the police and MI5 as they are extremely small.

c They can be used to make secret films of people without their knowledge, which is morally wrong.

Webcams can encourage online flirting with people who are married, which could destroy a marriage.

Teacher comment

a All the ticks are in the correct places so all three marks are given here.

b Both of these are advantages of webcams, so full marks for this part.

c Both of these answers are valid and so full marks are awarded.

(7 marks out of 7)

Answers

a One mark for each correctly placed tick:

	Tick **three** boxes
Watching the evolution of dinosaurs	
A parent checking up on their children in a nursery when they are at work	√
Looking at live video of an erupting volcano in a geography lesson	√
Watching a movie star constantly wherever they go	
Watching the space shuttle taking off as it happens	√

b One mark for each of two advantages such as:

They can record criminals and be used as evidence.

You can see what the weather is like in a resort you are soon to visit.

They are very cheap to buy.

You can chat with people and see them at the same time.

They are small and so can be hidden easily so people do not know you are looking at them.

Webcams mean that you can have a simple meeting without the need to travel.

People can view things in distant places that would be difficult for them to visit in person.

c One mark for each of two disadvantages such as:

The images from webcams are often poor quality.

It can make it easy for others to spy on you without you knowing.

It can invade people's privacy.

Topic 3

Storage devices and media

WORKED EXAMPLE

A presentation that contains multimedia features such as images, sound and video is to be transferred between computers.

a Give the names of **two** storage devices that can be used to store the files and explain why they are suitable for this application. *(4 marks)*

b All storage devices and media have disadvantages. For each storage device/media you have named in (a) state **two** disadvantages. *(2 marks)*

Sample answer 1

a CD – because lots of different files can be stored and all computers come with a CD drive

DVD – because the storage capacity is high and they work with all computers

b CD – you cannot store data on both side of the disk

DVD – the surface of this disk can easily be damaged which causes them not to work

Teacher comment

a Just stating either CD or DVD will not gain marks. As the presentation has been created on one computer and needs to be transferred to a different computer, there needs to be a write facility, so it is necessary to give the names DVD-RW or CD-RW.

In other questions where the write facility is not needed, the proper terms DVD-ROM or CD-ROM should be used rather than CD or DVD.

No marks for part (a)

b The lack of storage on both sides could (loosely) be considered as a limitation. The problem here is that the top surface tends to get scratched and also where would you put the label? Optical media is easily damaged so part (b) is an acceptable answer.

(2 marks out of 6)

Sample answer 2

a CD-RW – because the data can be recorded onto a CD-RW disk that has a high storage capacity that is ideal for all the multimedia files. Also all computers have a drive that is capable of reading the data off the disk.

Flash drive – the drive can be used just like another drive and has a high enough capacity to hold all the files needed and it is easy to transport being small in size and light.

b CD-RW – you have to take care when handling them as it is very easy to scratch the disk surface and prevent the CD-RW from being able to transfer data.

Flash drive – the access time is lower than that for an internal magnetic hard drive which means the data takes longer to load.

Teacher comment

a This answer identifies suitable storage devices/media and has clearly related their reasons to the transfer of multimedia files for a presentation. This part gains full marks.

b Two disadvantages of each storage media/device have been identified so full marks for this.

(6 marks out of 6)

Answers

a One mark for each device and one mark for the reason × 2.

Pen drive - small size means easily transferred from one computer to another

Pen drive - can be used by all computers as it simply plugs into the USB port/socket

Pen drive - can get cheap storage capacity which is enough for large music, animation, image files needed for a multimedia presentation

CD-RW - has a large storage capacity, which is needed because multimedia files are usually large

CD-RW - small in size which means they are easily transferred between computers

CD-RW - can be read by any computer with a CD drive or a DVD drive

b One mark for each disadvantage. Note the disadvantages must refer to the named storage devices in part (a).

CD-RW - easily scratched which causes read problems

CD-RW - limited amount of storage capacity

Pen drive - low access speed/transfer rate compared to a magnetic hard drive

Pen drive - easily bent and broken when in the USB port

Pen drive - often left in the machine by mistake and lost

Topic 4

Networks and the effects of using them

WORKED EXAMPLE

A small lawyers' office has ten stand-alone computers. They have been told that it is much more effective if all the computers are formed into a network.

State **three** benefits that the organisation would gain from networking their computers. *(6 marks)*

Sample answer 1

They would be able to access the internet.

They would be able to send email to each other without using the internet, which would be cheaper.

They could all use the same data.

Teacher comment

The first sentence is not strictly true. Stand-alone computers can, of course, access the internet. What they probably meant to say is that by networking the computers together they could all share a single internet connection.

The second sentence is true and well explained because they could still send email to each other using the internet but this can compromise the security of the data, so organisations like to send email internally without using the internet.

The last sentence is worth one mark.

(3 marks out of 6)

Sample answer 2

Using a network they are able to share resources such as printers and scanners. This means that they need only buy one of each rather than one for each computer, which will be much cheaper.

Any computer will be able to access files stored on the server. This means it will not be necessary for data to be copied so that it can be transferred between the computers.

All the computers will be able to share a single internet connection. This will be cheaper as all they need to buy is a router and they can then only pay for a single fast connection.

Teacher comment

This is a very well-structured and well-thought-out answer. Note how they have sectioned their answer. The first sentence introduces the benefit and then extra sentences add further explanation.

This good technique has helped this student gain all the marks for this question.

(6 marks out of 6)

Answers

One mark for a statement of the benefit and one mark for an explanation of the benefit × 3:

- Ability to share files (1) - no need to make copies of files as all the files can be accessed by all the computers on the network if needed (1).
- Ability to share hardware resources (1) - no need to have a printer for each computer as any hardware device (e.g. printer, scanner, plotter, etc.) can be shared (1).
- Ability to share software (1) - software can be shared, meaning that everyone will be using the same version. Maintaining software by keeping it up-to-date is made much easier (1).
- Lower software costs (1) - it is cheaper to buy one network version with a licence for so many users than to buy individual copies for each computer (1).
- Improved security (1) - it is easier for network managers to control access to the internet (1).
- Can share an internet connection (1) - one connection can allow all users access (1).
- Easier to back up files (1) - backing up is performed by the network manager rather than the individual users, which means backing up is taken seriously and users are less likely to lose data (1).
- Improved communication (1) - networks have email facilities, which will improve communication between workers (1).
- Central maintenance and support (1) - new upgrades to software need only to be added to the server and not to each computer (1).

Topic 5

The effects of using ICT

WORKED EXAMPLE

Working with computers is known to cause a number of health problems such as backache. Give the names of **two other** health problems that could arise through the use of computers, and in each case describe a precaution a user could take in order to help prevent it. *(4 marks)*

Sample answer 1

Backache because if you slouch in your chair you will get it.

Stress as too much work makes you stressed.

Teacher comment

The question has not been properly read. The question mentions 'backache' and states that '**two other**' health problems are needed so no marks for the first part.

The second answer could apply to work in general, not necessarily using computers, so this does not get a mark.

(0 marks out of 4)

Sample answer 2

Repetitive strain injury caused by prolonged use of a keyboard or mouse. You can help prevent it by adopting the correct posture by sitting up straight in your chair whilst using the computer.

Headaches caused by glare on the screen. The sun shining on the screen can be prevented by using adjustable blinds on the windows.

Teacher comment

This is a very good answer as it clearly states the condition and what can be done to help prevent it.

(4 marks out of 4)

Answers

One mark for the medical condition and one mark for a method of helping to prevent it from occurring.

Headaches (1) - use an antiglare screen (1)/use window blinds to reduce glare (1)/take regular breaks (1).

Eye strain (1) - use an antiglare screen (1)/use window blinds to reduce glare (1)/take regular breaks (1).

Repetitive strain injury (1) - maintain correct posture in chair (1)/use a straight-backed chair (1)/take regular breaks (1).

Topic 6

ICT applications

WORKED EXAMPLE 1

1 **a** Define what is meant by a robot. *(2 marks)*

b Robots are used in industry for a variety of tasks.
Give **two** tasks that robots are often used for in industry. *(2 marks)*

c Give **three** advantages in using robots in industry. *(3 marks)*

Sample answer 1

1 **a** A robot is a device like a human which walks around and talks.

b For spraying cars

For welding panels on cars

c You do not need to pay them so they are cheaper.

They can do the job better than a person because they do not have off days.

They work hard all the time not like humans who can be lazy.

Teacher comment

1 **a** This sounds more like the type of robot seen on Star Wars or in children toys. Robot is a key word so it would have been better to revise a definition.

No marks are given for this answer.

b The answer should have given more detail and mentioned 'for spraying cars with paint'. However, they were not penalised for this.

Both of the answers here were awarded a mark.

c All the answers here are correct so this part gains full marks.

(5 marks out of 7)

Sample answer 2

1 **a** It is a device that can be programmed to do a particular task such as assemble parts of a car engine. If you want the robot to do a different task, then you have to reprogram it.

b For welding the spouts on electric kettles

For packing goods in boxes ready to be sent to customers

c Robots can work continuously for long periods.

The robots can work 24 hours a day 365 days per year.

Once you have paid for them, the costs to keep them working is very low compared to employing staff.

Teacher comment

1 **a** This is a good answer that tells the examiner that robots can be programmed and that they are capable of being reprogrammed. The fact that robots can be reprogrammed makes them robots and not simply automatic devices such as a washing machine. Full marks are given for this answer.

b Both are jobs performed by robots so full marks are given again.

c The first two points made are almost the same so only one mark is given. It is always worth checking that your answers are distinctly different.

The second point is worth a mark.

(6 marks out of 7)

Answers

1 **a** One mark for each of two points such as:

A machine that can be programmed

To perform a series of actions

And is capable of being reprogrammed to carry out different actions or a different task

b One mark for each task to a maximum of two marks:

Paint spraying

Welding panels

Assembling components

Moving goods around a factory

c One mark for each advantage to a maximum of three marks.

Robots do not get tired or distracted.

Robots do not have to be paid.

They are capable of working 24/7.

They can work in dangerous conditions.

They are consistent and produce high-quality work.

They can create some new jobs such as the people who maintain or program them.

WORKED EXAMPLE 2

2 Medical expert systems are used by doctors.

a Describe the **four** parts of every expert system. *(4 marks)*

b Describe, using examples, **two** advantages of using an expert system in medicine. *(2 marks)*

Sample answer 1

2 **a** Database

Inference engine

GUI

b It enables an inexperienced doctor to do the job of a consultant.

It saves time.

Teacher comment

2 a 'Database' is not correct. The correct answer is 'knowledge base' which consists of factual knowledge and information about making good judgements. GUI (graphical user interface) is one type of interface that can be used as the interface between the user and the system. However, the correct answer is 'user interface' so this mark would not be given.
One mark for the correct answer 'Inference engine'.

b There is no way the inexperienced doctor becomes a consultant through using an expert system. Expert systems are only used in a small area of medicine, usually to aid diagnosis. 'Saving time' on its own, gains no marks. The answer should have said in what way the system saves time.

(1 mark out of 6)

Sample answer 2

2 **a** Knowledge base

Inference or reasoning engine

User interface

Rules base

b They can base their diagnosis on a lot more facts than a human can.

They will go through steps that a human expert may forget to take to arrive at a more accurate diagnosis.

Teacher comment

2 a All correct answers here. Both the answers 'Inference or reasoning engine' are correct.

b Both of these answers are distinctly different and correct, so full marks for this part.

(6 marks out of 6)

Answers

2 a One mark each to a maximum of four for:

Knowledge base

Inference engine

User interface

Rules base

b One mark each to a maximum of two marks for:

It leaves doctors/specialists more time to concentrate on serious cases.

The knowledge base can be kept more up-to-date.

Ordinary doctors can use the system to make an expert diagnosis without needing to contact a specialist.

There is faster diagnosis for patients so patients get better quicker.

It is cheaper to use the expert system than train doctors in the specialist area.

A human may forget to consider a certain fact, but the expert system will consider all the facts to arrive at a correct diagnosis.

WORKED EXAMPLE 3

3 Many people now choose to bank online because of the time savings it offers. They do not have to travel to the bank and then probably queue up.

There are other advantages of online banking. Discuss the other advantages and possible disadvantages to the bank customer. *(6 marks)*

Sample answer 1

2 Quicker – it is much quicker to use online banking.

Easier – you can sit at home and do it.

Safer – you can pay money without the need to draw cash out to pay bills.

The worry of hackers accessing your bank account may make it not worth your while having an online account.

Teacher comment

3 This question asks you to 'discuss' the advantages and disadvantages. This means that you are expected to answer in sentences and not simply give a list of points.

In addition to this, this answer has fallen into the trap of using the words 'quicker' and 'easier' without saying why.

There are no marks for the first three points.

The last point is made in a sentence and this is a valid disadvantage.

(1 mark out of 6)

Sample answer 2

3 Online accounts often give the best rates of interest because the bank's operating costs are lower than high street banks.

Customers do not have to waste time travelling to banks and queuing up to do simple transactions that they could do from home.

Customers no longer have to store their own paper bank statements as they can all be viewed online.

Goods are often bought by mail order or over the internet.

It is possible to pay by transferring money to another person's account using online banking which saves having to write a cheque or reveal credit card details.

Some customers will be worried about unauthorised access to their online account by hackers who could commit fraud.

Teacher comment

3 This is written in full sentences and they have discussed more than four correct advantages/disadvantages in detail. The explanations given were very clear.

(6 marks out of 6)

Answers

3 Advantages

A customer can move money between current and savings accounts quickly in order to take advantage of better rates of interest.

Customers can check all their statements online rather than have to store paper statements.

Online accounts frequently have better rates of interest.

You can pay bills or put money directly into another account from your home.

Online accounts offer 24/7 access so you can bank outside normal banking hours.

There is no paperwork with account numbers on to discard so there is reduced risk of identity theft.

You can apply for loans, overdrafts and credit cards without having to visit a bank.

It allows you to pay for goods and services without using cash or cheques, which is easier.

Disadvantages

Online bank accounts could be hacked into and your money stolen.

You cannot get cash so you still need to visit a cash machine.

Older people may prefer the personal service offered by a conventional bank.

WORKED EXAMPLE 4

4 A cutter in a clothing manufacturing company is controlled by a computer. The cutter is used to cut various patterns in cloth automatically using the following instructions.

START	means start program
CUTTER UP	means raise the cutter up
CUTTER DOWN	means lower the cutter down
FORWARD 10	means forward 10
BACKWARD 5	means backward 5
RIGHT 90	means right turn 90 degrees
LEFT 45	means left turn 45 degrees
CLEAR SCREEN	means clear screen
END	means end program

The cutter always starts with the cutter up so that it does not start cutting. When the END command is used the cutter will automatically return to its starting position.

a Write a program using instructions similar to the above that will cut out the shape shown here:

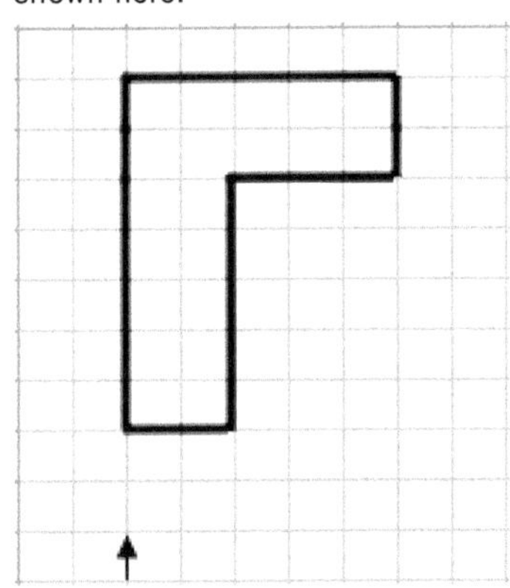

(3 marks)

b On the blank grid drawn below draw the shape that the cutter will cut out when carrying out the following program.

START
FORWARD 6
CUTTER DOWN
FORWARD 3
RIGHT 90
FORWARD 7
RIGHT 90
FORWARD 7
RIGHT 90
FORWARD 2
RIGHT 90
FORWARD 4
LEFT 90
FORWARD 5
CUTTER UP
END

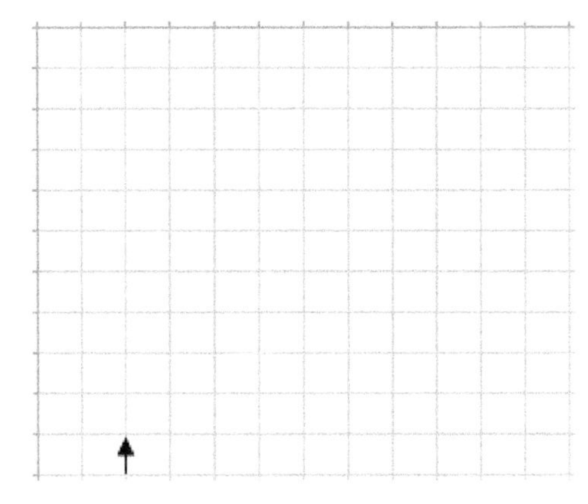

(2 marks)

c Give **two** reasons why it would be difficult for the cutter to cut out a complex shape using only those commands given above. *(2 marks)*

Sample answer 1

4 a FORWARD 7
RIGHT 90
FORWARD 5
RIGHT 90
FORWARD 2
RIGHT 90
FORWARD 3
LEFT 90
FORWARD 5
RIGHT 90
FORWARD 2
END

b

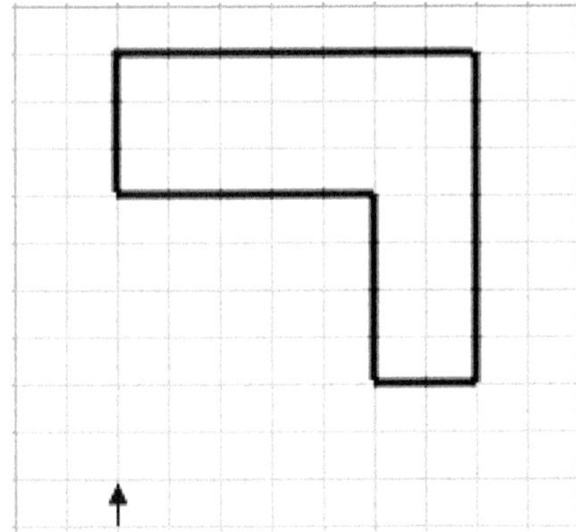

c You can't go diagonally because the diagonal distances are more than one square You can only go in straight lines

Teacher comment

4 a There is no start command instructing the computer to start obeying the set of instructions. Also the answer is from where the shape starts and not from where the tip of the arrow is. There is also no instruction CD telling the cutter to go down and start cutting. The middle section of commands is correct but the student has failed to raise the cutter before the END command. Only one mark is given for the middle section of correct commands.

b The correct shape has been drawn for the instructions so full marks (i.e. 2 marks) are given.

c These are both valid reasons so two marks here.

(5 marks out of 7)

Sample answer 2

4 a FORWARD 2
CUTTER DOWN
RIGHT 90
FORWARD 2
LEFT 90
FORWARD 5
RIGHT 90
FORWARD 3
LEFT 90
FORWARD 2
LEFT 90
FORWARD 5
LEFT 90
FORWARD 7
CUTTER UP
END

b

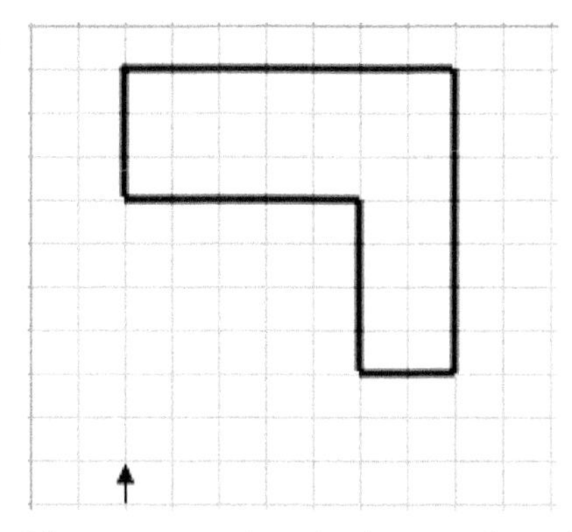

c You cannot give the instructions for curves.
Although you can move through angles it would be hard to know what distances to choose.

Teacher comment

4 a Most people would take a clockwise path around the shape but this student has decided to go anticlockwise. This is perfectly OK and these instructions will correctly cut the shape so three marks are given.

b The shape drawn on the grid is correct, so a full two marks here.

c Both reasons are correct so two marks are awarded.

(7 marks out of 7)

Answers

a One mark for all Box 1 steps correct

One mark for all Box 2 steps correct

One mark for all Box 3 steps correct

This is only one of the many possible answers. There is another correct answer given in sample answer 2.

START
FORWARD 2
CUTTER DOWN
FORWARD 7
RIGHT 90
FORWARD 5

RIGHT 90
FORWARD 2
RIGHT 90
FORWARD 3
LEFT 90
FORWARD 5

```
RIGHT 90
FORWARD 2
CUTTER UP
END
```

b

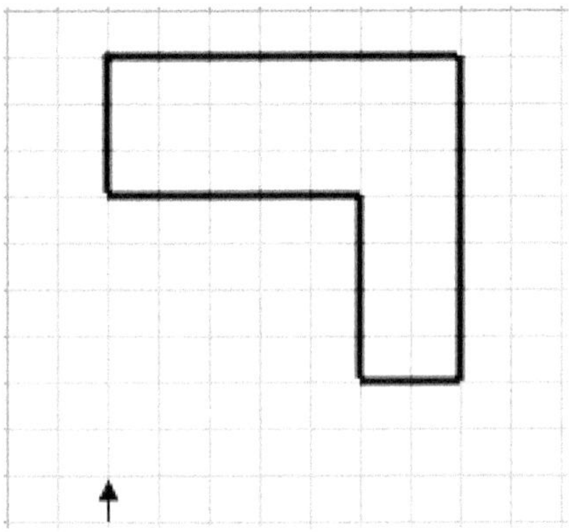

One mark for this section correctly drawn

START

FORWARD 6

CUTTER DOWN

FORWARD 3

RIGHT 90

FORWARD 7

RIGHT 90

One mark for this section correctly drawn

FORWARD 7

RIGHT 90

FORWARD 2

RIGHT 90

FORWARD 4

LEFT 90

FORWARD 5

CUTTER UP

c One mark for each one to a maximum of two marks:

The cutter can only travel in straight lines.

You cannot cut a smooth curve.

The diagonal distances are not known, so it is difficult to move the cutter accurately through an angle.

Topic 7

The systems life cycle

WORKED EXAMPLE

When a new system is produced it should be thoroughly tested. A testing plan is produced that uses normal, extreme and abnormal data. This test plan is carried out during the development and testing stage.

a Give one reason why a system should be tested. *(1 mark)*

b A test plan is created in the development and testing stage of the systems life cycle. Explain what is meant by a test plan. *(1 mark)*

c Explain what is meant by each of the following:

i Normal data *(1 mark)*

ii Extreme data *(1 mark)*

iii Abnormal data *(1 mark)*

Sample answer 1

a To make sure it works

b It is a plan that tests all the parts of the system.

c **i** This is just ordinary data that you input. It is not too big or small and will not be rejected by the system.

ii This is data that is too big or small and should be rejected by the system.

iii This is data that is just on the border of what is acceptable.

Teacher comment

a This is far too vague for a mark. Most systems will 'probably work' but a user wants a system to work without any errors. No marks for this answer.

b This simply repeats the words in the question. No marks here.

c **i** This is just about OK for a mark.

ii This is an incorrect definition so no mark here.

iii The answer is getting mixed up here with extreme data. No marks.

(1 mark out of 5)

Sample answer 2

a To make sure that the system works as expected by performing a number of tests

b The test plan includes lists of which tests are to be carried out with data to test and what should happen to the data when it is entered.

c **i** This is data that should be accepted by the system for processing.

ii This is data that is on the borderline of what is acceptable.

iii This is data that is completely incorrect and should be rejected by the system.

Teacher comment

a This is a good answer and gains one mark.

b This is a very good description of a test plan and gains one mark.

c **i** This is an acceptable answer so one mark is awarded.

ii This is a good answer so one mark.

iii Another good answer so one mark.

(5 marks out of 5)

Answers

a One mark for an answer such as:

Testing involves performing a series of checks to ensure that the system works as expected.

b One mark for an answer such as:

A detailed list of checks to be performed to test the system.

c **i** One mark for an answer similar to the following:

This is data that will pass all the validation rules and will be accepted for processing.

Alternatively, an example can be given:

Mark greater than or equal to 0 and also less than or equal to 100, so a typical piece of data would lie in this range.

ii One mark for an answer similar to the following:

It is a piece of data on the borderline of what is accepted.

Or a clear example such as:

For example, if an exam mark can be from 0 to 100 then 0 and 100 are examples of extreme data.

iii One mark for an answer similar to the following:

Data that is outside the validation checks and should be rejected by the system.

Topic 8

Safety and security

WORKED EXAMPLE

Computer viruses are a threat to computer systems.

a Explain what is meant by a computer virus. *(2 marks)*

b Give **one** thing that a computer virus might do on a computer system. *(1 mark)*

c Give **one** way of preventing computer viruses entering a system. *(1 mark)*

Sample answer 1

a A program that does damage

b Destroy the computer

c Use McAfee to stop viruses getting into your computer

Teacher comment

a This is a bit vague because it is not specific about what it does damage to. Only one mark is given for this answer.

b Viruses can be removed and therefore cannot be said to 'destroy' the computer. No marks for this.

c Brand names should never be given. So instead of McAfee they should have said 'antivirus software'. No marks are given for this answer.

(1 mark out of 4)

Sample answer 2

a It is a mischievous program that copies itself onto your computer and does harm by messing up settings or deleting data.

b It can start to make your computer run slow and can also cause it to crash unexpectedly.

c Use antivirus software to scan for viruses and remove them if they are found.

Teacher comment

a A good answer which makes it clear that it is a program that copies itself, so this answer is worth two marks.

b Again another good answer, which gains one mark.

c This answer is correct and gains one mark.

(4 marks out of 4)

Answers

a Two marks allocated in the following way:

Program that copies itself automatically (1) and causes damage to data or causes the computer to run slowly (1)

b One mark for an answer such as:

Can erase files which means the operating system software cannot be loaded

Can cause the deletion of data

Can cause the computer to crash

Can cause the changing of settings, which causes annoyance to the user

Can copy passwords and usernames and transmit these to another person

c One mark for one of the following:

Don't open file attachments unless you know who they are from.

Install antivirus software.

Keep antivirus software up-to-date.

Don't download files from unknown sources.

Topic 9

Audience

WORKED EXAMPLE

The internet is not policed although legislation is enforced in some countries.

a Give **one** effect of not policing the internet. *(1 mark)*

b Give **two** reasons the internet should be policed. *(2 marks)*

c Describe why policing the internet would be very difficult. *(4 marks)*

Sample answer 1

a You can get a lot of naughty material such as pornography which anyone can get.

b Children should not be able to access the material so it should be against the law.

There is lots of illegal stuff such as where to buy drugs.

c Everyone watches pornography so you cannot arrest everyone.

You would need loads of police and they are too busy arresting murderers.

Teacher comment

a The free availability of pornography is correct although some internet service providers can filter it out. *(1 mark out of 1)*

b These two points, although not expressed very well, are correct. *(2 marks out of 2)*

c The first answer is not true but the numbers would be large so this is worth a mark.

Some sites promote terrorism and police take many of the crimes seriously so this is not quite worth a mark.

(4 marks out of 7)

Sample answer 2

a You can find out how to do all sorts of things such as how to grow drugs or commit crimes.

b People should not be free to do what they want on the internet such as spread viruses.

They should be prosecuted if they send spam which wastes people's time.

c The police don't have enough staff to investigate internet misuse.

Lots of the misuses come from other countries so you would need lots of cooperation between police forces.

Teacher comment

a This is correct and worth a mark.

b Spreading viruses is illegal in most countries and some of the methods used to send spam are illegal. It is difficult to prosecute people who do these things. There is some policing in the two areas mentioned so this answer is only worth one mark.

c Both these answers are correct so worth two marks.

More detail could have helped this answer gain the full four marks.

(4 marks out of 7)

Answers

1 a People can set up pornographic sites, sites promoting drug use, sites promoting hacking, etc. with the knowledge that they probably will not be investigated or prosecuted.

b Films and TV programmes are policed, so the internet should be.

There is a lot of undesirable information on the internet such as how to grow drugs, how to make explosives, etc. and this information should be removed.

c It would be difficult because what is illegal in one country is legal in another.

Policing the internet would need agreement from all countries and this would be almost impossible.

The internet is global and it may be difficult to define which country's laws should be applied to the content.

Policing the internet would take up too many resources.

Topic 10

Communication

WORKED EXAMPLE

A software developer is working as part of a team of ten who are developing new software for an online loans company. The team members work in different parts of the country. The developers need to keep in touch with each other and need to pass work (mainly programs, screen designs, etc.) to each other.

a Explain **three** advantages of the developers contacting each other by email rather than by post. *(6 marks)*

b Describe **two** facilities provided by email software that will make it a lot easier to work as a team. *(4 marks)*

Sample answer 1

a Cheaper
Faster
Better

b Being able to send the email to more than one person
Being able to attach a file to an email

Teacher comment

a The word 'explain' means that a one word answer is not enough. There are 6 marks allocated here. One mark will be allocated to the clear explanation of the advantage with the other mark for the brief explanation of how it relates to working in teams. Avoid general words like 'better'. You need to be specific. General words such as 'faster', 'cheaper', 'better' gain no marks.

(0 marks out of 6)

b 'Being able to send the email to more than one person' is a facility of email software, but there needs to be a fuller explanation as to how this facility will make things easier when working as a team. It is important to tailor answers to the information given in the question.

Again 'Being able to attach a file to an email' is a facility provided by email software. There needs to be further elaboration on why this is an advantage.

(2 marks out of 4)

Sample answer 2

a Sending emails speeds things up. An email can be sent and replied to in seconds, whereas a letter sent and replied to takes several days.

It is cheaper, as there is no cost for paper, printing, envelopes and stamps.

It is faster to send an email and get a reply.

b It is possible to create groups and send the same email to all the members of the group rather than send each email separately.

They can attach other files to the email such as programs and screen designs and this avoids them having to save them onto removable media such as a flash drive.

Teacher comment

a The first two answers are good answers and would get full marks.

The third answer is almost a repeat of the first answer. It is always important to check your answer is not similar to an answer already given.

(4 marks out of 6)

b Both answers are good and gain full marks.

(4 marks out of 4)

Answers

a Any three advantages (two marks each) such as:

- Email is cheaper than a letter. No stamp, envelope or paper is needed. There is also a time saving, so this makes email cheaper. Even if the email is sent across the world, it will not cost any more than a local email.
- Quick to write. They are informal, meaning that people do not spend time on the layout, and the odd spelling mistake is acceptable.
- Ideal if there is a time difference. The reader can check email when they are ready.
- Inexpensive and easy to send the same email message to lots of different people.
- You can attach a copy of the sender's email with your reply, so this saves them having to search for the original message.
- You do not have to go out to a post box, so it saves time.
- You do not have to shop for stamps, envelopes and paper.
- Fast. It takes seconds to send and receive email. If the person at the other end checks their email regularly, then a reply can be sent very quickly.

b Two facilities (two marks each) such as:

- Groups/distribution lists – allowing you to send the same email to a group of people without having to select individual email addresses.
- File attachments – being able to attach files to an email so others can download the work onto their own computers and can comment on it.

Topic 11

File management

WORKED EXAMPLE

Ahmed is sending Jessica a large database file which has been created in different software than the database software that Jessica uses. It has been suggested that Ahmed saves the file in a generic file format and compresses the file before attaching it to an email and sending it.

a Explain what is meant by a generic file format. *(2 marks)*

b Explain the reasons why Ahmed compressed the database file before sending it to Jessica. *(2 marks)*

Sample answer 1

a It is a file that everyone can use. You can use it even if you don't have the software.

b You can't send big files using email.

Teacher comment

a This answer is too vague.
(0 marks out of 2)

b The question asks for reasons but this answer only gives one.
(1 mark out of 2)

Sample answer 2

a A generic file format is a format that lots of different software can save files in and lots of software can read and then use the files in. It is useful if you need to send a file created in certain software and the person does not have the same software.

b File compression makes the file size smaller which means it will send faster.

Teacher comment

a This is a good answer and makes the main points.
(2 marks out of 2)

b It is good that the answer mentions the reduction in the file size but sending it faster is a bit vague as it should mention the method by which the file is sent. So, if this had said 'sending the file to another person as a file attachment to an email' then this would have been worth a mark. Also only one answer is given.
(0 marks out of 2)

Answers

a Two marks as follows:

File format that is not restricted to use by a particular piece of software (1)

File formats that different pieces of software can save in or read from (1)

They can be used to transfer files between different pieces of software (1)

b Two marks as follows:

A method of reducing the file size (1)

So that the file can be sent over the internet/across a network in less time (1)

So more of the files can be saved in the same space on the storage medium (e.g. photo image files on a memory card) (1)

To enable the file to be attached to an email and sent as there is often a limit on the size of a file that can be sent in this way (1)

Topic 18

Databases

WORKED EXAMPLE 1

1 A school keeps details of all its students on a computer. Part of the data is shown below. The data is structured in fields, records and files.

Student_Number	Surname	Forename	Date of birth	Form
1211	Lee	Jaccck	12/11/06	11T
1225	Hughes	Amy	34/08/06	11G

a Explain these terms:

i Field

ii Record

iii File *(3 marks)*

b The data contained in the above structure contains two mistakes. One of these mistakes could have been discovered by a verification process and the other mistake by a validation process.

Fill in the table shown below by explaining what the mistake is and whether verification or validation could have detected the mistake, and describe a method which could be used to prevent the error. *(6 marks)*

Description of mistake	Discovered by verification or validation?	Description of method which could have been used to prevent the mistake

Sample answer 1

1 a i The information about a thing or person

ii A row in the table

iii The whole lot of information about a thing or person

b

Description of mistake	Discovered by verification or validation?	Description of method which could have been used to prevent the mistake
Wrong date of birth 34/08/06 is impossible as the days in August only go up to 31.	Validation	Range check on the days in the date to ensure it is equal to or less than 31
Forename has wrong name entered. Jaccck should be spelt Jack.	Verification	Use a spellchecker to make sure that the name is spelt correctly.

Teacher comment

1 a i This answer defines a record here instead of a field. No marks.

ii This answer is a bit brief but worth one mark. A more complete answer would be to say that it is the details about a person, thing or transaction. An example would be the detail about one student, which is a row in the table.

iii This statement is a bit vague so no mark is given. If they had given an example, such as a collection of all the records about students in the school, then this would have been clearer.

b The first row of answers is all correct. The last answer about a range check is OK, but if you allocate a data type of Date to a field then you cannot enter an impossible date.

The second row contains a typing error and it is not always appropriate to use spellcheckers with the names of people. The first two answers are correct for a mark each but the last answer gains no marks.

(6 marks out of 9)

Sample answer 2

1 a i A field is an item of data or fact about a student. Date of birth is an example of a field.

ii A record is a collection of fields about a person or thing. In this case it is the information about a particular student.

iii A file is a complete collection of records and would be the complete records of every student in the school.

b

Description of mistake	Discovered by verification or validation?	Description of method which could have been used to prevent the mistake
Incorrect date of birth 34/08/06 This is an impossible date	Validation	Use format check for the date field. Once this is set, the user has to enter the date in a certain format e.g. DD/MM/YY.
Typing error. Jaccck should be spelt Jack.	Verification	Use a visual check to compare the data. Check by reading the entered data on the screen and correct any mistakes.

Teacher comment

1 a i This is a good answer and notice the way the answer refers to the data in the table as an example. One mark for this.

ii Another good answer gains another mark.

iii Again another mark.

b The answers to all the parts to this answer are clear and show good understanding of the terminology. Full marks are given for this part.

(9 marks out of 9)

Answers

1 a i One mark for a definition such as:

A field is an item of data such as surname, date of birth, etc.

ii One mark for a definition such as:

A record is a collection of fields about a person or thing.

A line in the table about one particular student is a record.

iii One mark for a definition such as:

A file is a collection of records which forms the complete set of information about a thing or person.

The details of all the records of all the students in a school is a file.

b One mark for each correct answer in the table to a maximum of six marks.

Description of mistake	Discovered by verification or validation?	Description of method which could have been used to prevent the mistake
Invalid date/wrong number of days for the month/cannot have more than 31 days in a month	Validation	Use Date format/set data type to Date Use a range check/restrict day to 31 or less
Typing error/transcription error Jaccck should be Jack.	Verification	Use a visual check/proofread/get person who is the data subject to check their record. Double entry of the data.

WORKED EXAMPLE 2

The manager of a tool hire company wishes to use a relational database to help keep track of the business. The database stores the data in three tables, called: Tools, Customers and Rentals.

2 a Explain what a relational database is and what its main features are. *(5 marks)*

b What are the main advantages to this manager in storing the data in a relational database rather than a flat file database? *(3 marks)*

Sample answer 1

2 **a** A relational database is a database that has relationships between it. The relationships mean that you can get all the data out of the database in whatever order you want. Relational databases are proper databases and are good for businesses that use them a lot.

b The manager will be able to access the data from lots of different places.

To put the data into the relational database requires less typing as you only need to put the data in one file.

The manager will be able to find out information such as which customer has which tool.

Teacher comment

2 a The first sentence could be thought up by anyone using the term 'relational database' so it gets no marks. To obtain the marks, they would need to mention that the relationships are links formed between tables.

The other sentences are vague statements and this student obviously knows little about these databases. No marks are awarded for this part of the answer.

b The first sentence seems to be getting mixed up with distributed databases. The second sentence is a main advantage in using relational databases and therefore gets one mark. The third sentence is not specific and is awarded no marks.

(1 mark out of 8)

Sample answer 2

2 **a** A relational database consists of a collection of data organised into different tables with each table containing a set of data that is relevant to the organisation. Three tables would be used here: a customer table, a tool table and a rentals table.

The data is put into the separate tables but the tables are linked together, so it is possible to combine the information from data in all the tables.

b He won't have to type as much in as there is not as much duplication of data as there would be with a flat file.

If a customer changed their address then with a flat file the manager would have to change the address in each current record where a piece of equipment has been hired. This means that if a customer has hired five different pieces of equipment the address would need changing five times.

Teacher comment

2 a There are three separate points made here so three marks.

b This answer mentions duplication of data and easier updating process and has explained each of these well. Two marks are given here.

(5 marks out of 8)

Answers

2 **a** One mark each for five features of a relational database.

Note they must be features and not advantages.

- Databases that do not store all the data in a single table.
- They use several tables.
- Tables are linked together (or mention of relationships).
- Data in one table can be combined with data in any of the other tables.

b One mark each for three distinctly different advantages that must be relevant to this application.

- Full customer details do not need to be entered when a customer who has rented before rents again.
- If a mailshot needs to go out to customers, the manager will not need to go through all the orders extracting names and addresses as you can use the Customer table.
- An update is easier to make as the manager will only need to alter the data once in one of the tables.
- The data is stored more efficiently, so it will be faster to do searches and sorts.
- There will be fewer data errors since the data is only entered once, which means the manager can rely on the information produced.

Topic 19

Presentations

WORKED EXAMPLE

1 A presentation is to be used by visitors to a castle. The idea is that users will be able to find out about the history of the castle and what it was like to live in a castle in that era.

Explain how each of the following could be used in the design of this presentation.

a Animations *(2 marks)*

b Links *(2 marks)*

c Slide transitions *(2 marks)*

Sample answer 1

a Use moving things

Makes it better

b You can move from one slide to another.

The user can click on a hot spot.

c The material on the slide can shoot in from the side of the slide.

It makes it exciting for the user.

Teacher comment

a This is a vague and poor answer and no marks are awarded.

b Both of these are valid answers and one mark is awarded for it.

c Material such as bullet points shooting onto the slide is not really an example of slide transition as the slide is already on the screen. One mark (just) is given for the second answer.

(2 marks out of 6)

Sample answer 2

a Use moving images showing what is in each room.

Have a heading showing the names of the castle which moves from left to right.

b Allow the user to decide what they want to see next by allowing them to click on links which take them to other pages.

Links could be used to allow the user to virtually visit each of the rooms and look around.

c These are pictures around the edge of a slide.

You can sometimes find these included with clip art.

Teacher comment

a These are both suitable examples so two marks are awarded.

b These two very good answers explaining how links might be used are awarded two marks.

c What the student has described here are borders. Slide transitions are the way one slide is removed and the next slide appears. No marks for this answer.

(4 marks out of 6)

Answers

a One mark for each point (it must be a sensible use of animation) to a maximum of two marks.

Have a cartoon showing what life was like

Use animation to show how certain parts of the castle were used

etc.

b One mark for each point to a maximum of two marks.

Link to an aerial view such as Google Earth

Link to other pages in the presentation

Link to the internet so that they can access further information

etc.

c One mark for each point to a maximum of two marks.

Have one slide fading as another slide appears

Have one slide shooting in from the side

etc.

Topic 20

Spreadsheets

WORKED EXAMPLE

1 Yasmin has started work after leaving university and has to live away from home. She has recorded her wages and costs into a spreadsheet and this is shown here.

	A	B	C	D	E	F	G	H	I	J
1	Month	Wages	Electricity	Gas	Phone	Rent	Clothes	Food	Total costs	Money left over
2	Jan	£1,500	£60	£55	£62	£210	£40	£600	£1,027	£473
3	Feb	£1,520	£60	£55	£65	£210	£40	£600	£1,030	£490
4	Mar	£1,550	£60	£55	£64	£210	£40	£600	£1,029	£521
5	Apr	£1,550	£60	£55	£50	£210	£40	£600	£1,015	£535
6	May	£1,680	£60	£55	£47	£210	£40	£600	£1,012	£668
7	Jun	£1,690	£60	£55	£47	£210	£40	£600	£1,012	£678
8	Jul	£1,730	£60	£55	£53	£210	£40	£600	£1,018	£712
9	Aug	£1,742	£60	£55	£54	£210	£40	£600	£1,019	£723
10	Sep	£1,800	£60	£55	£62	£210	£40	£600	£1,027	£773
11	Oct	£1,800	£60	£55	£44	£210	£40	£600	£1,009	£791
12	Nov	£1,800	£60	£55	£39	£210	£40	£600	£1,004	£796
13	Dec	£1,745	£60	£55	£53	£210	£40	£600	£1,018	£727
14										

a Which one of the following formulae could be used to work out the **Total costs** in cell **I2**?

A =SUM(I2:I13)

B =I2+I3+I4+I6+I7+I8

C =SUM(B2:H2)

D =B2+C2+D2+E2+F2+H2+I2 *(1 mark)*

b Give a suitable formula that could be entered into cell J2 to work out the money Yasmin has left over at the end of the month. *(1 mark)*

c The cells apart from cells in column A and row 1 have been formatted.

Which of the following types of cell formatting have been used for these cells?

A Euros

B Calculation

C Currency

D Right align *(1 mark)*

d Labels are important in spreadsheets. Give the cell reference of a cell containing a label. *(1 mark)*

e Give two advantages of Yasmin using a spreadsheet such as this to help her budget her money. *(2 marks)*

Sample answer 1

1 **a** D

b B2-I2

c C

d A1

e It is quicker

It is more efficient

Teacher comment

1 **a** When adding up cells you do not include the cell where the answer is to be put so this answer is wrong.

b The respondent has forgotten to put the equals sign in front of this formula (i.e. =B2-I2). This small point has cost a mark here.

c This is correct so one mark here.

d A label is any cell which describes data on the spreadsheet, so this is correct and gains one mark.

e Not a strong answer. It should have said in what way is it quicker and in what way is it more efficient. No marks for either of these answers.

(2 marks out of 6)

Sample answer 2

1 **a** C = SUM(B2:H2)

b =B2-I2

c C Currency

d Row 1

e Provided the calculations have been set up correctly and tested, the formulae will always produce a correct calculation.

When one of the numbers in the spreadsheet is changed, the cells which depend on the changed cell will recalculate automatically.

Teacher comment

1 **a** This is correct so one mark here.

b This is correct so one mark here.

c This is correct so one mark here.

d All the cells in row 1 do contain labels but the question asks for a cell reference, so this is an incorrect answer so no marks.

e These are both very good answers and worth a mark each.

(5 marks out of 6)

Answers

1 **a** One mark for the letter, formula or both (i.e. C = SUM(B2:H2))

b One mark for a correct formula which must include the equals sign (i.e. =B2-I2).

c One mark for C Currency.

d One mark for any cell reference in row 1 or column A. It must be a cell reference and not a column letter or row number.

e One mark for each of two advantages of a spreadsheet such as:

If set up correctly, the formulae will always produce a correct calculation.

Automatic recalculation when numbers are changed in the spreadsheet.

Once the spreadsheet has been set up, the spreadsheet can be reused for different years by putting in different data.

The data can easily be represented pictorially by getting the spreadsheet to produce graphs and charts.

You can change the information in the spreadsheet in order to make and test 'What if' scenarios.

Revision material

The following material will help with revision for the theory paper.

Worksheet R1

Can you work out what the word is?

Here are some words or phrases which have been jumbled up. The words are connected with software. Can you work out what they are? There is a clue to help you.

1 desert phase

Hint: Software good for manipulating numerical data.

Answer: ______________________________

2 progress cod win

Hint: Software you would write a letter with.

Answer: ______________________________

3 shipbuild kept song

Hint: Software good for combining text and graphics.

Answer: ______________________________

4 patient snore

Hint: Software used to present material on slides.

Answer: ______________________________

5 plastic piano

Hint: Type of software used to do a specific job.

Answer: ______________________________

6 generosity stamp

Hint: Software that controls the hardware directly.

Answer: ______________________________

Worksheet R1 (continued)

7 **romp rag**

Hint: Step-by-step instructions.

Answer: ____________________

8 **abase tad**

Hint: Software that puts data into a certain structure.

Answer: ____________________

9 **woodland**

Hint: Obtaining software using the internet.

Answer: ____________________

10 **ray poll**

Hint: Program used for working out wages.

Answer: ____________________

Worksheet R2

The internet

What do these terms mean?

Here is a list of terms in alphabetical order. Write the meanings next to the term. If you don't know what the meaning is, then use one of the glossaries available on the internet.

Term	Meaning
Browser	
Cookie	
Download	
Email	
FAQ	
HTML	
Hacker	
ISP	
Link	
Surfing	
User-ID	
Web page	

Theory: Revision questions

1 Here are some different methods of entering data into a computer:

OMR **MICR** **magnetic stripe** **barcodes**

keyboard **sensors** **voice recognition** **mouse**

Using the list above, choose the best method of data capture for each of the following situations:

a For inputting credit or debit card details when customers are paying for goods in a supermarket

____

b To use with a graphical user interface

____

c For obtaining temperature measurements in a greenhouse

____

d For recording the answers on a multiple-choice answer sheet

____

e For dictating a story directly into a word processor

____

f To record the details of items being sold in a supermarket

______________________________ [6]

2 Place a tick in the boxes that contain tasks performed by the operating system of a computer.

Task	Put a tick here if the task is performed by the operating system.
Performing calculations in a spreadsheet	
Managing space for files on the disk drive	
Issuing an instruction to the printer to start printing	
Formatting text in a word-processed document	
Accepting the input from a mouse	
Spellchecking a document	
Copying a file from one disk to another	

[4]

3 Hospitals make use of ICT systems for keeping patient records. Apart from contact details such as name, address, postcode and telephone numbers, give **four** distinctly different fields that would be included in a patient database and describe why they are needed.

____

____

____

____

____

____

____

____

[8]

4 Loyalty schemes are very popular in stores for encouraging shoppers to make purchases at the store on a regular basis. When customers join the scheme they fill in an application form and when this is done, the details are entered into a database and a plastic card containing a magnetic stripe is sent by post to the customer.

When customer details are entered into a database they are verified and validated.

a Define the term verification. Name and describe **one** verification method that can be used during the entry of customer data.

[3]

b Define the term validation. Name and describe **one** validation method used during the entry of customer data.

[3]

5 Here are some descriptions of methods of verification and validation. You have to state whether each one represents verification or validation.

a Two operators typing the same data in twice. Only if the data is exactly the same, will it be accepted for processing.

[1]

b Making sure that an employee number is entered into a field before the payroll details can be processed.

[1]

c Checking an order after it has been typed in by reading the paper order and seeing if it is exactly the same as what is on the screen.

________________________ [1]

d A program that makes sure that the amount for a gas bill is not ridiculously large.

________________________ [1]

6 Tick (√) the correct column to show whether each of the following statements about health risks in using ICT is true or false.

	True	False
The continual use of keyboards over a long period can give rise to aches and pains in the hands, arms and wrists.		
RSI stands for repeated stress injury.		
Wrist rests and ergonomic keyboards can help prevent RSI.		
Backache can be caused by slouching in your chair when using a computer.		
Glare on the screen can cause RSI.		

[5]

7 It is important to fully document a system. For each of the following types of system documentation, put a tick in the relevant box to indicate whether it is technical or user documentation.

	Technical	User
Test plans		
Trouble-shooting guide		
Program coding/Program listing		
File structures		
Frequently Asked Questions (FAQ)		
System flowcharts		
How to log in and log out of the system		
The hardware requirements to run the system		
Tutorials to explain how to use the system		

[9]

8 A heated greenhouse in a normally cold country is being used to grow tropical fruit. They want the growing conditions inside the greenhouse to be controlled automatically using a computer.

a Give the names of **three** sensors that they would need to use to measure the soil and growing conditions.

____

____

[3]

b Output devices will be needed to control the growing conditions. Describe **three** output devices that they would need to control the growing conditions.

____

____

____

____

____

[3]

c Describe the computer processing which would be required to maintain the necessary growing conditions.

____
____
____
____
____
____
____
____

[5]

d Computers are used to control the conditions inside the greenhouse. Explain why computers are used rather than humans for this purpose.

____
____
____
____

[3]

9 A small network is to be created in a home so that all the computers can share files and an internet connection. Explain why each of the following devices would be needed.

A router ____
____

A browser ____
____

Email ____
____

An ISP ____
____

[4]

10 Many people use the internet for booking holidays and theatre tickets as well as for banking. Discuss this development and explain the effect it is having on ordinary people and their lives.

____
____
____
____
____
____
____
____
____
____
____
____

[8]

11 The internet has allowed many new services to be developed. Two such services are vlogs and wikis.

a Give **two** features of a wiki.

____

____

[2]

b Give **two** features of a vlog.

____

____

[2]

12 Describe the differences between a LAN and a WAN.

____

____

____

____

____

____

____

____

____

[5]

Answers

Worksheet R1
Can you work out what the word is?

1 Spreadsheet
2 Word processing
3 Desk top publishing
4 Presentation
5 Applications
6 Operating system
7 Program
8 Database
9 Download
10 Payroll

Worksheet R2
The internet

Term	Meaning
Browser	Software used to search for information using the internet
Cookie	A small program which monitors your searching activity
Download	Obtaining a file off the internet and saving it on your own computer
Email	An electronic message sent over a network which is usually the internet
FAQ	Frequently Asked Questions. A list of the questions the people who use a website most often ask, along with the answers
HTML	A list of instructions on how to display the content of a web page
Hacker	A person who gains illegal access to a computer system
ISP	Internet service provider. The people who provide you with your internet connection
Link	A way of moving from one place to another on the internet
Surfing	Moving around different web pages and websites using the links on the internet
User-ID	A name given to you or that you give yourself so that you are recognised by the system
Web page	A document/page which has been uploaded to enable it to be accessed by anyone using the internet

Theory: Revision questions

1 One mark for each correct answer:

- a Magnetic stripe
- b Mouse
- c Sensors
- d OMR
- e Voice recognition
- f Barcodes

2 One mark for each correctly placed tick.

Task	Put a tick here if the task is performed by the operating system.
Performing calculations in a spreadsheet	
Managing space for files on the hard disk	√
Issuing an instruction to the printer to start printing	√
Formatting text in a word-processed document	
Accepting the input from a mouse	√
Spellchecking a document	
Copying a file from one folder to another	√

3 One mark for the name of the field and one mark for the correct description. Candidates must supply a sensible field in the context of a patient record and a correct explanation. Any contact details for the patient gain no marks.

DOB – so that their age can be calculated – important when calculating dosages of drugs

Next of kin – in case they need to be contacted about deteriorating condition, death, etc.

Allergies – so doctors can ensure certain drugs are not given that the patient is allergic to

Medication – doctors can see the drugs the patient is taking to make sure suitable drugs are prescribed

Current GP – so the family doctor can be contacted with information about the patient's treatment

Patient number – used to identify a particular patient to the computer system

Operations – details of any operations the patient has had in their lifetime so the doctors are able to make a correct diagnosis

Medical conditions – doctors treating one medical condition will need to know other conditions the patient suffers from

4 **a** One mark for a suitable definition such as:

Verification means checking that the data being entered into the ICT system perfectly matches the source of the data.

No mark for the name of the method but up to two marks for the description.

Proofreading/visual check – carefully reading what they have typed in (1) and comparing it with what is on the data source/application form to find errors (1).

Double entry of data – two people use the same data source to enter the details into the database (1) and only if the two sets of data are identical, will they be accepted for processing (1).

b One mark for a suitable definition such as:

Validation – the process which ensures that data accepted for processing is sensible and reasonable.

No mark for the name of the method but up to two marks for the description.

Presence checks – some database fields have to be filled in whilst others can be left empty (1) so if data for an essential field is left blank, the data for the other fields will not be accepted for processing (1).

Data type checks – check if the data being entered is the same type as the data type specified for the field (1). This would check that only numbers are entered into fields specified as numeric (1).

Range checks – performed on numbers to check that a number being entered is within a certain range (1). For example, if you have to be over a certain age to have a loyalty card then if a date of birth were entered and this gave an age less than this, the data entry would not be allowed by the range check (1).

Format checks – performed on codes to make sure that they conform to the correct combinations of characters (1). For example, a date of birth may have to be in a certain format (e.g. dd/mm/yy) and unless it is in the correct format it will be rejected (1).

5 One mark for each correct answer.

a Verification

b Validation

c Verification

d Validation

6 One mark for each tick placed in the correct column.

	True	False
The continual use of keyboards over a long period can give rise to aches and pains in the hands, arms and wrists.	√	
RSI stands for repeated stress injury		√
Wrist rests and ergonomic keyboards can help prevent RSI	√	
Backache can be caused by slouching in your chair when using a computer	√	
Glare on the screen can cause RSI		√

7 One mark for each tick placed in the correct column.

	Technical	User
Test plans	√	
Trouble-shooting guide		√
Program coding/Program listing	√	
File structures	√	
Frequently Asked Questions (FAQ)		√
System flowcharts	√	
How to log in and log out of the system		√
The hardware requirements to run the system		√
Tutorials to explain how to use the system		√

8 **a** One mark for each of three sensors from:

Moisture

Humidity

Temperature

Light

pH

Gas (oxygen or carbon dioxide)

b One mark for each description:

Buzzer – to warn if the conditions go outside the ideal conditions (e.g. if the temperature is too low).

Heaters – will turn on if the temperature is too cold and turn off if it is too hot.

Air conditioner – will cool the greenhouse down if it gets too hot.

Light bulb – will supply artificial light if the outside light intensity falls.

Motors – will open the windows if the humidity is too high or the temperature is too high and close if they are too low.

Fan – used to reduce the temperature if it gets too hot.

c Maximum of five points from:

A temperature sensor continually monitors the temperature and sends a reading to the processor at regular intervals.

It is compared with a stored value to see whether it is too high or low.

If the temperature is lower than the stored value then a signal is sent to the heater to switch it on.

If the temperature is lower than the stored value then a signal is sent to the motor to shut the windows if they are open.

If the temperature is higher than the stored value then a signal is sent to the heater to switch it off.

If the temperature is higher than the stored value and the windows are shut then a signal is sent to the motor to open them.

If the temperature is higher than the stored value then a signal is sent to turn on the fan.

A light sensor continually monitors the light level and sends a reading to the processor at regular intervals.

The light level is compared with the stored value.

If the light level is less than the stored value the processor sends an instruction to turn the light on.

If the light level is greater than the stored value and the light is on, then an instruction is given to turn it off.

A moisture sensor continually monitors moisture readings and sends a reading to the processor at regular intervals.

The moisture level is compared with the stored value.

If the moisture level is too low an instruction is sent by the processor to switch on the sprinkler.

If the moisture level is too high and the sprinkler is on then the processor turns the sprinkler off.

d Three explanations from:

The computer can control the conditions 24 hours per day.

It is cheaper as humans do not have to be paid to control the conditions.

The response time of the computer is faster so it is able to control the conditions more accurately.

Computers can take readings more frequently.

9 One mark for each correct answer:

A router – enables all the computers in the network to share a single link to the internet

A browser – software that can be used to find and display web pages and to access resources on the internet

Email – method of sending digital messages from one person to another

An ISP – an organisation which supplies users with a permanent connection to the internet

10 Eight from:

Advantages

Do not have to waste time travelling to banks/shops/travel agents/theatres

Disabled people can gain their independence because they do not have to rely on others

Less pollution as fewer car journeys are needed

Much greater choice of products/holidays to choose from

Can book/shop/bank 24/7

Do not have to queue up to pay for goods/services

No travelling expenses (e.g. fares, petrol, car parking)

Disadvantages

No social interaction

Not everyone has a computer or connection to the internet

Hackers may gain access to your credit card/banking details

Some sites are bogus and are used to steal your money

If you buy clothes you have the hassle of sending them back if they do not fit or suit you

You cannot get the goods immediately because you usually have to wait for delivery

There is no personal touch

Can only have a maximum of 5 marks from either advantages or disadvantages.

11 **a** One mark each for two points:

A wiki is a web page.

It can be viewed and modified by anyone who has a web browser.

b One mark each for two points:

A personal website or social media account where a person regularly posts short videos of themselves, for example reviewing a product or an event.

They are interactive and allow a visitor to leave comments.

12 One mark for each difference to a maximum of five marks:

LAN is confined to a small area/WAN covers a wide geographical area such as between cities, countries, etc.

LAN is located in a single building or site/WAN covers lots of buildings such as branches.

LAN uses cable, wireless, infra-red and microwave links which are usually owned by the organisation, whereas WANs use expensive telecommunications equipment such as satellite links.

LANs are cheaper to build as the organisation owns the networking equipment. WANs are more expensive because of the cost of services from telecoms companies.

LANs have lower speed connections because the amount of data transferred across the network is small. WANs have high amounts of data transfer so need fast connections.

LANs are cheaper to run as they are simple, whereas WANs need specialist staff who are highly paid.

Exam-style question paper

1 Hardware is the physical components of computer systems.

Circle **three** items which are examples of computer hardware.

antivirus software	operating system	PIN pad	compiler
pressure sensor	web browser	scanner	linker

[3]

2 Direct data entry is used to enter certain items of data into a computer system. Write the name of the input device making use of direct data entry that is most appropriate for the entry of the following items of data:

a The shaded boxes on a survey form

b The sort code and account number that is pre-printed in special ink at the bottom of a bank cheque

c Debit card details when paying for a bill in a restaurant

d Reading data at a distance when a library book is returned at a drop-off point when the library is closed [4]

3 Tick true or false next to each of these statements:

	True	False
System software is always a single program.		
Compilers can be part of systems software.		
Compilers convert program instructions written in a high-level computer language to binary.		
Linkers are part of system software.		

[4]

4 An oven is being used to heat a meal.

a The microwave oven uses several pre-set variables.

i Explain what is meant by a pre-set variable. [1]

ii Describe two pre-set variables which have to be pre-set on the oven before the cooking starts. [2]

b A microprocessor controls the operation of the oven.
Describe how the microprocessor controls the operation of the oven. [6]

5 a Antivirus software should be installed on all computers. State the role of antivirus software and describe three functions carried out by antivirus software. [4]

b State the role of a firewall and describe three functions of firewall software installed on a network. [4]

6 A smartphone uses many methods for data input and output.

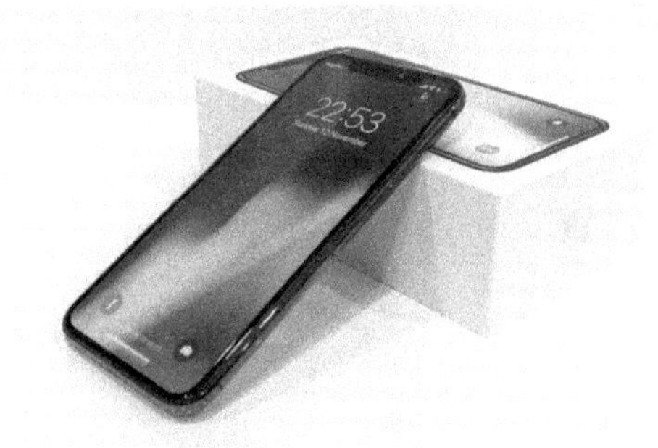

For each of the items listed below, tick the correct box to indicate if they are used for:

- input only
- output only
- input and output
- neither input nor output.

Item	Input only	Output only	Input and output	Not used for input or output
Microphone				
Touch screen				
Earphone				
Speaker				
Camera				
Memory card				
Volume button				

[7]

7 A model for a proposed school barbeque for charity was created using spreadsheet software.

The model shows the money coming in (called the income) and the money going out (called the expenditure). It also shows the profit they are likely to achieve which can be given to charity.

	A	B	C	D	E	F	G
1	**Year 10 and 11 Proposed Barbeque For Charity**						
2	**Estimated Income/Expenditure**						
3	Total No of tickets sold	200		Ticket price	£5.00		
4							
5	**INCOME**						
6	Ticket sales	£1,000.00					
7	Drink sales	£96.00					
8	Raffle ticket sales	£100.00		Total income	£1,196.00		
9				Total expenditure	£562.50		
10	**EXPENDITURE**			Profit	£633.50		
11	Hire of party lights	£27.00					
12	Hire of disco unit	£35.00					
13	Hire of barbeque	£45.00					
14	Barbeque fuel	£14.00					
15	Fire lighters	£4.00					
16	Food	£300.00					
17	Printing of tickets	£27.50					
18	Cases of soft drink (240 cans)	£60.00					
19	Raffle prizes	£50.00					
20							

a Explain what is meant by a computer model. [2]

b One of the advantages of a computer model is that you can find answers to questions such as 'What if I altered this?' By giving a suitable example using this model, explain what this means. [2]

c Write down the formula that could be used in each of the following cells to calculate their values.

i B6 [1]

ii E8 [1]

iii E9 [1]

iv E10 [1]

8 The following screenshot shows part of a flat file database that has been created using spreadsheet software to hold the details for a job agency.

	A	B	C	D	E	F
1	**Job Number**	**Job Type**	**Area**	**Employer**	**Pay**	
2	1010	Systems Analyst	London	Am Bank	£35,000	
3	1023	Programmer	Blackburn	Minstral Finance	£28,000	
4	1012	Accountant	Liverpool	Mutual Insurance	£42,000	
5	1034	Sales Clerk	Liverpool	Mutual Insurance	£18,000	
6	1011	Sales Manager	Birmingham	DC Switches Ltd	£28,000	
7	1045	Sales Manager	Lancaster	Air Products Ltd	£31,500	
8	1024	Electrical Engineer	Bristol	Manners Ltd	£27,800	
9	1021	Network Manger	Warrington	D&Q Ltd	£19,800	
10	1000	Trainee Programmer	Cardiff	PCSoft	£7,500	
11	1002	Systems Analyst	Liverpool	AmSoft	£24,000	
12	1013	Junior Accountant	Liverpool	AmSoft	£17,000	
13	1018	Accountant	Manchester	DC Switches Ltd	£45,000	
14	1035	Sales Clerk	Preston	FR Venn & Co	£16,900	
15	1078	Shipping Clerk	London	P&R	£21,800	
16	1080	Trainee Programmer	London	Arc Systems	£19,300	
17	1079	Programmer	London	Arc Systems	£35,600	

a Describe the differences between a flat file database and a relational database. [3]

b Give the name of the field that should be used as the primary key. [1]

c Write down the Job Number of the record selected using the following search conditions.

i Pay < £8000 [1]

ii Pay >= £35500 AND Area = 'London' [1]

d Write down all the Job Numbers of the records selected using the following search condition.

Job Type = 'Sales Clerk' OR Job = 'Shipping Clerk' [1]

9 An expert system is to be created which will help car mechanics with their diagnoses of faults in car engines.

Describe the steps involved in the design and creation of such an expert system. [5]

10 The RFID chip shown below is used in a passport, which is used to supply certain information about the person to whom the passport belongs at an automated border control.

a Describe two features of an RFID chip. [2]

b Describe how this passport containing the RFID chip is used when passing through an automated gate at border control. [3]

11 Tick true or false next to each of these statements:

	True	False
Backup copies are copies of programs and data kept for security purposes.		
Backup copies of data should always be kept on hard disk.		
Removable media or the cloud should be used for backup copies.		
Magnetic tape is always used for the taking of backup copies.		

[4]

12 Describe the differences between a router and a switch. [4]

13 Documents prepared and printed out using a computer and printer often contain a header or a footer or both.

a Describe the difference between a header and a footer. [2]

b Give **three** different pieces of information that would be put in headers or footers. [3]

c Explain the differences between proofreading a document and spellchecking a document. [3]

14 Dot matrix printer Laser printer Inkjet printer

Choose a printer from the list above which best fits each description.

a A very noisy printer

b The printer you would most likely use to print high-quality photographic images stored on your home computer

c A printer which is able to print multi-part stationery

d The only printer which uses an inked ribbon

e A printer which produces the lowest quality text

f The printer which uses ink in a toner cartridge [5]

15 Multi-national organisations with staff in offices all over the world make use of video-conferencing. Discuss the advantages and disadvantages of using video-conferencing to conduct meetings rather than using face-to-face meetings. [8]

16 A bank stores its customer details on a file server. This file server is connected to the internet so that customers can access their accounts online.

a Hackers could access the customer account details. Describe **three** ways a hacker could misuse the data. [3]

b Describe the purpose of **three** different authentication techniques. [3]

17 The following three layers are used in web development:

Content layer

Presentation layer

Behaviour layer

a Explain why three layers are used. [1]

b Describe what would typically be included in each of these layers. [6]

Answers to exam-style question paper

1 One mark each for:

PIN pad

Pressure sensor

Scanner

2 One mark each for:

a Optical mark reader

b Magnetic ink character reader

c Magnetic stripe reader/Chip and PIN reader

d RFID tag reader

3 One mark for each correct answer.

	True	False
System software is always a single program.		√
Compilers can be part of systems software.	√	
Compilers convert program instructions written in a high level computer language to binary.	√	
Linkers are part of system software.	√	

4 a i One mark for an answer similar to the following:

A pre-set variable is a variable that is set by the user of the system and is used as input to the system. The control system tries to keep the thing it is controlling at this pre-set value.

ii One mark for each of two pre-set values:

Temperature

Time/duration

b One mark for each of the following points to a maximum of six marks.

Microprocessor switches the oven on.

The timer is switched on.

The microprocessor obtains temperature readings from the temperature sensor.

The temperature value is compared with the pre-set value the user entered.

If the value is less than the pre-set value the heating element is turned on.

If the value is greater the heating element is turned off.

The time is continually monitored and compared with the pre-set value.

When the time has reached the pre-set time entered by the user, the oven is turned off.

On turning the oven off, a signal is sent to the buzzer which is sounded to alert the user.

5 a One mark for a definition similar to:

Software to detect and remove viruses

Software to prevent viruses from entering a computer system

One mark each for three functions such as:

Checking that emails coming in and out of the system do not contain viruses

Checking that files downloaded do not contain viruses

Performing regular scans on all hard drives

Maintaining an up-to-date database of all known viruses

Detecting suspicious activity that could indicate a virus infection

b One mark for a definition similar to the following:

A piece of hardware or software or both that is able to protect a network from hackers

One mark each for three functions such as:

Used to filter data packets

Used to block access to certain websites

Prevents access to the computer network from unknown IP addresses

Blocks software being run on the computer without the user's permission

Blocks certain downloads

6 One mark for each correctly placed tick.

Item	Input only	Output only	Input and output	Not used for input or output
Microphone	√			
Touch screen			√	
Earphone		√		
Speaker		√		
Camera	√			
Memory card				√
Volume button	√			

7 a One mark for an answer similar to the following:

A representation of a real-life situation using a computer program and making use of mathematical equations

b One mark for a suitable answer which shows the model being used, such as:

Determining the number of tickets you would need to sell in order to break-even (i.e. where the income equals the expenditure)

c i One mark for =B3*E3

ii One mark for =B6+B7+B8 or =SUM(B6:B8)

iii One mark for =E11+E12+E13+E14+E15+E16+E17+E18+E19 or =SUM(E11:E19)

iv One mark for =E8–E9

8 a One mark each for three points similar to the following:

Flat files only consist of one table of data.

Relational databases store the data in several tables.

Relational databases use links between the tables.

Flat file databases do not use links.

Flat files are only suitable for simple databases.

b One mark for: Job Number

c i One mark for 1000

ii One mark for 1079

d One mark for 1034, 1035 and 1078.

9 One mark for each of the following steps to a maximum of five marks.

Experts are interviewed.

Data is collected from experts.

Rules base is designed and tested.

Knowledge base is designed and tested.

Input and output format/screens are designed.

Expert system is checked by using known results.

10 a Two features (one mark each) from the following:

An integrated circuit/chip on which data is stored

An aerial

The aerial is used to send and receive data

b One mark for each of the following to a maximum of three marks:

Passport is opened and placed on a scanner/RFID reader.

Data on the RFID is read.

A scanner scans the passport holder's face/fingerprints.

Facial characteristics/fingerprints are compared with those stored on the RFID chip.

If there is a match, the barrier opens automatically.

11 One mark each for each correct answer.

	True	False
Backup copies are copies of programs and data kept for security purposes.	√	
Backup copies of data should always be kept on hard disk.		√
Removable media or the cloud should be used for backup copies.	√	
Magnetic tape is always used for the taking of backup copies.		√

12 One mark for each point to a maximum of four marks.

A switch is used to connect devices on a network together.

A router connects actual networks together (e.g. a LAN to a WAN such as the internet).

Routers use IP addresses to send packets of data to the correct destination.

Switches can learn or store the addresses of each computer in that part of the network where the switch is connected.

A router transfers data between networks.

A switch transfers data between devices (e.g. computers and devices that are part of the network).

A router can be used to connect a network or computer to the internet.

13 a One mark for:

A header is an area between the top of the page and the top margin into which information can be typed.

A footer is an area between the bottom of the page and the bottom margin into which information can be typed.

b One mark each for three of the following:

Page numbers

Today's date

The title

A company logo

The author's name

The filename of the document

c One mark for:

Spellchecking is mainly performed by the computer.

Proofreading is mainly performed manually.

Spellchecking checks a word is spelt correctly but it does not check that the word is used in the correct context.

Proofreading checks the format of the document.

Proofreading checks for consistency in the document.

Proofreading checks that sentences make sense.

Proofreading checks for factual errors in what is being written about.

14 One mark for each correct answer.

a Dot matrix printer

b Inkjet printer

c Dot matrix printer

d Dot matrix printer

e Dot matrix printer

f Laser printer

15 One mark for each of the following points:

Advantages

Meetings can be called at short notice

Not as much planning is needed to hold meetings

No travelling expenses need to be paid

More family friendly as employees do not need to spend time away from home

There are no hotel or venue expenses

No time wasted travelling

Some employees may be scared to fly/travel

Disadvantages

The equipment required is expensive

It takes time to train people to use the equipment

Time differences can make holding meetings difficult

You cannot pass around a product/prototype using video-conferencing

You cannot sign legal documents using video-conferencing

The bandwidth can be a problem in certain areas/countries

Some people communicate better if there is personal contact

16 **a** One mark for each answer to a maximum of three marks.

The hacker could find embarrassing information which could be disclosed to others.

The hacker could deliberately delete or alter information.

The hacker could use their card details to make online purchases.

The hacker could transfer money to their own account.

The hacker could take out new loans fraudulently.

b One mark for each authentication technique to a maximum of three marks.

Combination of usernames and passwords. The username identifies the person to the system and the password ensures it is them and not someone pretending to be them. Sometimes memorable data is also used which only the user will know.

The use of biometric methods which use a unique property of the human body to recognise a person, e.g. fingerprint, pattern on retina or iris, face recognition.

Use of a smart card with a chip so that people without the card cannot access the system.

Use of a magnetic stripe card which needs to be swiped in order to access the system.

17 a One mark for a description similar to the following:

Because different skills sets are needed to create and design each of the layers enabling all layers to be worked on at the same time.

b One mark for each of two items in each layer.

Content layer

Text

Images

Video

Sound/narration

Presentation layer

Design of the pages

Creation of cascading style sheets

Behaviour layer

Creation of the HTML

Creation of links between pages

Revision tips

Here are some revision tips which will hopefully help you to maximise your mark in the examinations for both theory and practical.

In the student book, Topics 1 to 10 cover the theory aspects of the Cambridge IGCSE® Information and Communication 0417 syllabus. There may be some questions on communication, spreadsheets, databases and other material in the theory paper, but you will gain the knowledge needed by attempting all the practical work.

The material for the practical papers is covered in Topics 11 to 21 of the student book.

How do I revise?

Everyone has their own way of revising but here are a few tips which might help:

- Start your revision early. Remember you will have lots of other subjects to revise nearer exam time.
- Work at a table or desk with bright light.
- Work somewhere quiet where there will not be any distractions.
- Write brief notes out. You tend to remember more of what you write compared to what you read.
- Make a plan of how much revision you will do and the times you will do it. Try to stick to this.
- Try to get up early. If you complete your revision, you have the rest of the day to enjoy yourself.
- Get friends/relatives to test you. You could give them the glossary at the back of the book to test you on definitions of terms.
- Read carefully the following tips and remember to apply them in an examination.
- Print a copy of the syllabus out. You can get a copy from the Cambridge International Examinations website. Use this as a good summary of what you have to learn. Many students like to highlight the material using a pen when they have thoroughly understood the material.
- Learn all the facts, terms and concepts in the syllabus.
- Do not simply memorise the material as you may have to apply the concepts to a situation asked in a question.
- There are many questions in the student book, including many Cambridge IGCSE past paper questions. You can test yourself by answering them and then marking them yourself using the answers which are supplied in the *Teacher Resource Pack* which your teacher is likely to have.
- Use your teacher/lecturer. If you do not understand something, do not be afraid to ask them.
- Use past papers, some of which can be obtained from the Cambridge International Examinations website, to help you revise. You will also be able to obtain some mark schemes for the examination from the website. Your teacher will be able to supply you with recent past papers and mark schemes. The more you understand about the way these papers are marked, the more marks you are likely to achieve in your examinations.
- Make sure that you understand the differences between the command words used on the examination papers. These words include name/give/describe/discuss/explain.

Before an exam

Here are some things you should do on the days of the examinations:

- Collect the necessary equipment: two pens (in case one dries up); two pencils; a sharpener; a rubber; and a ruler.
- Always take a watch into the exam. There will be a clock in the exam room but if you are at the back you might not be able to see it.
- Go to the toilet before the exam; this avoids the embarrassment of having to leave the room under supervision.
- Check to see if you have to wear school uniform.

Tips for the theory paper

- Always read the instructions on the front of the paper carefully. In particular, note the time you are allowed. Read the question carefully before answering. Ensure that your answer is the answer to the precise question being asked. Too many students see a key word and then write everything they know about it.
- Do not write any irrelevant information in answer to a question. You will not gain marks and simply penalise yourself by the time you waste.
- Allocate your time sensibly. Use the mark scheme at the side of the questions as a guide to how much you should write. If there are, say, two marks, there must be two points you need to mention in order to get both marks.
- Try to write neatly. The examiners have hundreds of scripts to mark and might miss some important information in an answer if they cannot decipher an illegible script.
- Only do what the question asks. If it asks for two reasons, make sure that you give two: not three or one. Always check that in an answer to a question with two parts, you have not written similar answers to both parts. If you have, you will only obtain marks for one of them.
- After you have answered a question, read it through again to make sure that you have not missed part of it out.
- Make sure that you answer all the questions on the paper. If you leave a question out to answer later, you must remember to go back to it.
- Do not give your answer as a series of notes or bullet points. Your answers should be given, where appropriate, in complete sentences.
- If a question asks you to give an example in an answer then not giving an example will cost you marks.
- Read the whole question carefully before you start to answer. This is to avoid giving too much information in one of the answers which should have been given as an answer to a later part of the same question.

Understanding what the question means

There are certain command words used in questions and it is important to understand what they mean. If you write too much you will waste time. If you write too little you will be likely to lose marks. You need to write the correct amount. Here is what each command word means.

State

Express in clear terms.

Give

Here you have to provide the person marking the question with more information than a single-word statement.

Describe

This means that you should give a detailed answer. If there are four marks allocated, then make sure that you write a minimum of four sentences with each covering a different aspect of the answer. You have to convince the person marking the question that you can describe an answer that is appropriate to the question.

Define

This usually means explain a technical term in language that anyone could understand.

Explain/Give reasons

Explain means saying why certain things happen as opposed to describing what happens. You need to give an answer in sentences here and ensure the reasons why something happens are clear. If you simply say what happens, you might not get the marks available.

Discuss

Discuss usually involves writing down both the advantages and the disadvantages to show both sides of an argument in a given situation. As well as doing this, you should also come to a conclusion.

The practical papers: things you must do when submitting your work for the practical exams

- Make sure that you obey the instructions on the paper.
- Make sure that your name and other details, such as candidate number, as specified on the exam paper are included on every printout you produce. If you do not put your name on a printout it will not be marked.
- If you have a printout which you do not want to be marked, you must cross out the work.
- You will probably practise the practical work by completing previous examination papers. This is a good idea but you must not rely on the examination paper you do being similar to a previous one. You must be able to adapt your knowledge of software and the practical skills you have gained to new situations.
- Read the paper carefully from start to finish before starting to complete the questions. This will give you an overview and you can think about the skills you will need to use in your answers.